The Permanent Revolution PLAYBOOK

APEST for the People of God:
A six week exploration

by Alan Hirsch & Tim Catchim

A MISSIO
PLAYBOOK

Producer: Matt Smay
Designer: Peter Schrock, assistance from Kevin Tracy and Kate Cozzie
Editor: Robert Neely and Samizdat Creative

©2014 Missio Publishing
Published by Missio Publishing
ISBN 978-0-9899578-2-3
Printed in Canada

All Scripture quotations, unless otherwise indicated, are taken from the Holy Bible, New International Version®, NIV®. Copyright ©1973, 1978, 1984, 2011 by Biblica, Inc.™ Used by permission of Zondervan. All rights reserved worldwide. www.zondervan.com The "NIV" and "New International Version" are trademarks registered in the United States Patent and Trademark Office by Biblica, Inc.™

Scripture quotations marked (ESV) are from The Holy Bible, English Standard Version® (ESV®), copyright © 2001 by Crossway, a publishing ministry of Good News Publishers. Used by permission. All rights reserved.

Scripture quotations marked (NLT) are taken from the Holy Bible, New Living Translation, copyright © 1996, 2004, 2007 by Tyndale House Foundation. Used by permission of Tyndale House Publishers, Inc., Carol Stream, Illinois 60188. All rights reserved.

CONTENTS

// Introduction

INTRODUCTION

More Than You Can Imagine...

Ephesians contains one of the most bountiful promises relating to community and discipleship in all of Scripture. *"Now to him who is able to do immeasurably more than all we ask or imagine, according to his power that is at work within us, to him be glory in the church and in Christ Jesus throughout all generations"* (Ephesians 3:20-21). This scripture says that Jesus' church will be so great and transformative that it will not only exceed our imaginations, it will also be empowered to extend this transformative capacity from one generation to another right down through the ages. Envisaged here is nothing less than a revolutionary move of God that can keep going until its very purposes are fulfilled...In other words, *the church is meant to be a dynamic, transformative, permanent revolution!*

This promise is so challenging because most of us, if we are honest, would admit that our experience in the church is probably less than what can be termed "revolutionary." If one is inclined to think that the standard contemporary church experience fits the definition of revolutionary, then you have in all likelihood misunderstood the full implications of this piece of scripture. Paul says that God can do more than all we ask or imagine. This means whatever our experience is at the moment,it is too small—there is so much more.

So, if there really is more to church than the present reality, and it's part of the promise of the gospel, then why are we not experiencing it? If we are meant to be a permanent revolution that does previously unimaginable things from generation to generation, then what is stopping us? Why are we not being the kind of people Jesus clearly intended for us to be? What's missing? Well, Paul doesn't leave us without some clues. In fact, one such clue is found in the very next chapter of Ephesians. Let's take a look.

Designed for Permanent Revolution

One of the ways to understand our problem is to say that we are perfectly designed to achieve what we are currently achieving. In other words, our current experience of being less than revolutionary can be traced back, in large part, to the very ways we operate as the body of Christ.

The power and energy to become a permanent revolution is available to us, this much is clear from Scripture. But if we interfere with the original design of the body of Christ, then we should not be too surprised when we turn out being less than what was intended. It's kind of like removing the spark plugs from your car and replacing them with AAA batteries. Needless to say, your car is not going to function properly.

RADICAL UNITY

We believe Ephesians 4 lays out important, yet often overlooked, instructions as to how the church is to organize itself for ministry. So what is the original design? Paul starts off Ephesians 4 by laying the foundation for unity in verses 1-6:

As a prisoner for the Lord, then, I urge you to live a life worthy of the calling you have received. Be completely humble and gentle; be patient, bearing with one another in love. Make every effort to keep the unity of the Spirit through the bond of peace. There is one body and one Spirit, just as you were called to one hope when you were called; one Lord, one faith, one baptism; one God and Father of all, who is over all and through all and in all.

Paul not only addresses our posture towards one another, he also outlines seven "ones," giving the church its foundation as well as the framework of unity. These seven core doctrines help clarify the boundaries of orthodoxy for all times and places.

COACHING MOMENT

It's important to remember the difference between spiritual, relational and theological unity. Spiritual unity is not something that is achieved through our own efforts. Jesus has already created spiritual unity for those who are in Christ through his work on the cross (Eph 2:14-18). Our task is to recognize our spiritual unity in Christ and live according to this reality. Recognizing our spiritual unity in Christ helps us work towards relational unity (4:1-3). Theological unity is bringing our core beliefs into alignment with the core theological essentials in Scripture as in, for example, the seven ones. It is our spiritual unity in Christ that creates the environment for the diversity of personalities and giftings in the body to function, rooted in the core theological truths of scripture.

RADICAL DIVERSITY

Having laid out the basis for unity, Paul proceeds to affirm the Christ-apportioned nature of ministry in the church. The text says in verses 7 and 11:

But to each one of us grace has been given as Christ apportioned it...So Christ himself gave the apostles, the prophets, the evangelists, the pastors and teachers.

Paul is outlining in very simple terms the core ministries that make up the body of Christ. He clearly states that Christ has "given" certain gifts to "each one of us" and distributed them throughout the body as He sees fit. The ministry of the church is unmistakably stated as being at least five-fold in form. This five-fold form finds expression in the giftings of apostle, prophet, evangelist, shepherd and teacher (APEST). It is through the diversity of APEST that we are able to perceive and operate in the full spectrum of Christ's ministry.

RADICAL MATURITY

According to the text, these five giftings have expressly been given

...to equip his people for works of service, so that the body of Christ may be built up until we all reach unity in the faith and in the knowledge of the Son of God and become mature, attaining to the whole measure of the fullness of Christ. (Ephesians 4:12-13)

The word "equip" in this passage is an interesting word. It was often used to describe the setting of a broken bone (alignment). Paul is saying that each of the ministries within APEST somehow adds capacity to the rest of the body and helps it function properly. Our ability to grow and mature into the church that Jesus intended us to be is directly linked to the ministries within APEST.

Sadly, most churches have traditionally operated with only two out of the five: namely shepherding and teaching. In most cases, the ministries of the apostle, prophet and evangelist (APE's) have often been overshadowed, if not completely scripted out of the vocabulary and practices of the church. Essentially, we have cut off 3/5ths of our capacity to grow and mature!

By limiting the church's ministry and leadership primarily to shepherding and teaching, we have done serious damage to the church's ability to mature and be the fullness of Christ in the world. If only two out of the five ministries are operating in the body, then no wonder the church is not being the revolutionary force we are intended to be. We have been walking like someone with a broken leg, limping along, unable to function at full capacity.

During the weeks ahead, we will explore how to reactivate the full spectrum of Christ's ministry within your group. But just to make sure we are on the same page, let's start by defining some basic concepts and definitions.

Basic Concepts

CALLING OR VOCATION

Paul says in Ephesians 4:1 that we are to walk worthy of the *calling* which we have received. While the text says that Christ "gave" some to be apostles, prophets, evangelists, shepherds and teachers in verse 11, we believe the role of APEST is best described by using the language of calling or vocation. APEST represents ministry capacities that have been given to "each one of us." **They are not in the first instance leadership positions, titles or offices.** As we will discuss later, they are life-long callings (vocations) that are built in to the very core of how all of God's people are called and empowered by God (Ephesians 2:10).

PRIMARY GIFTING OR BASE MINISTRY

When describing the ways you are primarily gifted for ministry through APEST, we will often use the language of "primary gifting" or "base ministry." This is really just two different ways of saying the same thing.

APEST

The Apostle:
"One who is sent and extends"
The word apostle literally means "sent one." The Latin form of this word is *missio*, which is where we get our English word *mission* from. The apostle is the one most responsible to activate, develop and protect the sentness/purposes of church. This "sent" quality gives their life a catalytic influence, often playing the role of entrepreneur at the forefront of new ventures. They are cultural architects who are concerned with the overall extension of Christianity as a whole throughout culture and society. As such, they are often drawn to issues related to design, systems and overarching organizational structures. Above all, they have a missional (sent) focus to their ministry.

The Prophet:
"One who questions and reforms"
Prophets are sensitive to God and what is important to Him. They often have a sense of what truth needs to be emphasized for their time and place. Essentially, prophets are guardians of the covenant relationship. Whether it is in the church, society or some organizational setting, prophets are quick to recognize the gap between "what is" and "what should be." The weight of this tension leads prophets to question the status quo as well as initiate efforts of reform. Ultimately, they are not satisfied until they see a "closing of the gap" between God's demands and our covenantal faithfulness. This desire to see the truth of God's reality fleshed out in concrete and tangible ways gives an incarnational (enfleshed) quality to their ministry.

The Evangelist:
"One who recruits and gathers"
Evangelists communicate the message of the Good News in joyous, infectious ways. They tend to enjoy meeting new people and wooing them into a relationship. They are avid communicators of ideas and often share their thoughts and feelings in convincing ways. They are recruiters to the cause and find great fulfillment in helping people get caught up into the driving narrative of the church/organization—the Gospel of the Kingdom. As people who are bearers of good news, they have an attractional quality to their ministry.

The Shepherd:

"One who protects and provides"

Shepherds have a natural instinct to protect the community from danger and provide for its needs on both an individual and communal level. They often notice when people are alone or hurting, and feel drawn to nurture the spiritual and communal health of the church. They have a sense of loyalty to the organization and the people within it. They ensure the community is experienced as a safe and loving environment, giving their ministry a distinctly communal focus.

The Teacher:

"One who understands and explains"

Teachers find great satisfaction in helping people learn truth and wisdom. As the more philosophical types, they grasp complex, systemic truths and then help people understand them. They often formulate curriculum and pathways of learning. They ensure the truths of Scripture are passed along from generation to generation. Their ministry could be said to be primarily instructional in nature.

EQUIPPING

The word *equip (katartizmo)* in Ephesians 4 has several images attached to it. Sometimes it is used in reference to the setting of a broken bone. At other times it is used to describe the mending of broken fishing nets. In each case, the general idea is the same. To equip someone for works of ministry means you help them grow in their capacity to function in one of the APEST ministries. For example, apostles are given to the body so that they can equip the rest of the body (individually and collectively) to function apostolically. Prophets equip the body to function prophetically. Evangelists equip the body to function evangelistically, and so on down the list.

COACHING MOMENT

Equipping can take place organically through exposure to different environments created by each of the APEST ministries, respectively. Or it can happen in a more organized fashion through training courses, intentional relationships and structured environments where people are not just exposed to APEST, but experiment with serving in those five areas of ministry. The best kind of equipping includes both an organic and an organized approach.

MATURITY

Maturity in Ephesians 4 is primarily about growing in our capacity to function within all five APEST ministries. This kind of maturity is achieved at both an individual and a collective level. As each person both gives and receives training in their respective APEST ministry, the body grows individually and collectively in their capacity to represent the fullness of Christ.

FULLNESS IN CHRIST

In Ephesians 4, the phrase "fullness of Christ" describes the net result of our growth and maturity as a body. As APEST equips us (individually and collectively) to do what Jesus did, the church begins to not only grow in every way, it also begins to reflect to the world the full spectrum of Christ's character and ministry (4:15). APEST positions the church to actually start functioning and looking like Christ. When this happens, the full impact of Christ's ministry is reproduced through the church for the sake of the world.

PERMANENT REVOLUTION

In this *Playbook,* we will use the term *permanent revolution* to describe the impact that the church is designed to have on culture and society. It goes without saying that the word *permanent* implies an ongoing, perpetual state of affairs. We use the word *revolution* in its most literal sense. The word *volution* carries the idea of movement. As a sign and instrument of God's kingdom, the church is designed to be a continuous, unending, ever expanding force of transformation in the world—a *permanent movement.*

The Playbook

Just like all the other Missio Publishing resources, this *Playbook* is designed to introduce biblical principles in practical ways that facilitate individual and collective learning experiences. As a *Playbook,* it assumes the people going through this material are either currently or will potentially be doing ministry together as a group or team. It is a great resource to take an existing group through or as introductory material for groups that are just forming.

So whether you are currently in a group or are at the beginning phases of starting one, the *Permanent Revolution Playbook* has been especially designed to help develop a team's full potential for ministry and leadership. If you have taken a group through any of the *Missio Primers*, then this *Playbook* is an excellent way to expose potential or existing leaders that have emerged from that experience to valuable training materials and practices.

As a *Playbook*, it contains key principles, relevant scenarios and group exercises that will help your team flourish amidst the challenges of leading and doing ministry. Specifically, this *Playbook* is designed to help you:

1. Discover the nature and function of APEST for ministry and leadership
2. Identify your individual APEST ministry profile
3. Recognize APEST ministry giftings in your group, team or ministry
4. Function with greater levels of awareness and appreciation for how each person uniquely contributes to the growth and maturity of the body
5. Move towards greater levels of growth and maturity

Like any group exercise, you will only get out of it what you put into it. This

Playbook can facilitate learning and point you in the right direction, but it can't ultimately take your team where it needs to be. Team work is challenging, but the rewards are exponential if you are willing to put in the time and energy to experience a breakthrough.

How To Use This Playbook

Each daily element of the week is designed to facilitate a learning experience. Six of those days are designed to help you process individually, apart from your group or team. On the Synergy Day (Day 5) you will meet with your group to participate in a group learning experience. Here is a quick overview of what you can expect as you work through this *Playbook:*

Coaching Moments

Occasionally, we will add a tip in the *Coaching Moment* box. Sometimes this will add a helpful insight, sometimes it will serve as a reminder to make sure you get the most out your *Playbook* experience. Either way, do not skip this feature!

Day 1: EXPLORATION

The first day of the weekly rhythm will introduce the subject of the week. We'll provide Scriptures and overarching principles to frame your learning experience and give it direction. We'll also provide questions and journaling space so that you can wrestle with the realities of Ephesians 4 and what it means for you as a leader and for your team. Here's fair warning: the questions are not surface level. At times they will provoke tension and sustained reflection. This is all healthy and normal. Part of growing a ministry is learning how to work through differences while at the same time affirming your love and commitment to one another. Good groups know how to speak the truth—in love.

Day 2: MEDITATION

The meditation day helps you internalize the truths from Day 1 and reflect on how they cast new light on your situation. There will be a Scripture or two to soak in for a little while. Read it a couple of times and let it do its work in you. Don't forget the questions at the end. You may be asked to share your answers later on, so be sure to write them down in your *Playbook.*

Day 3: CHANGE

The Change Day is where you make an intentional effort to apply the principles of Scripture to the realities of your own life. What does this idea mean for your role as a follower of Jesus, as a leader, as a group member? How would this change your ministry for the better?

Day 4: ACTION

In the end, knowledge without action leads to an empty spirituality. Action Day is about putting developing practices that help us live into the implications of what we are learning. Every week has a personal action step for you to take. It's absolutely critical that you follow through with these assignments, so be sure to make time in your weekly schedule to complete those actions.

Day 5: SYNERGY
Every group or team needs to spend time encouraging and challenging one another. This is what makes groups effective. This is a day when you get together with the other members of your team and process what each of you have been learning. In our opinion, this day and the Action Day are the most important days of the week.

Day 6: CALIBRATION
On Day 6, we'll revisit the theme of the week from a different angle and give you some additional things to think about as you wrestle with the topic of the week and allow God to bring transformation into your life. This is a great time to process the insights and reflections that came up during your Synergy meeting the day before.

Day 7: RECREATE
The last day of your weekly rhythm is a day of rest. You get to listen, reflect and even celebrate what God has been doing throughout the past six days. What has God been doing in you? What has he been doing in your group? Taking time to rest in what He has already done ReCreates us and gives us the resources we need to move forward and face the challenges ahead. It is best to do Day 7 in a place where you can focus and contemplate without interruption.

Getting the Group Together

We have learned that it helps to give group members time to process the new content and work through its implications as an individual before processing it together. Before you begin this journey, pick a day your group will begin to meet. Before this first official meeting, give each member enough time to go through the first four days of Week 1. This will ensure everyone has had time to absorb and process the material, as well as participate in the Action day.

As we've already mentioned, we suggest this *Playbook* is best used in a group of people who are, or will be, engaged in ministry together in some form or fashion. We have found that it is good to limit the size of your group to a maximum of 12 people. Typically, a group this size can easily fit in most homes, apartments or coffee shops. It is large enough to accommodate the occasional absentee and small enough not to require a master coordinator to facilitate meals together.

What day will your group meet for a Synergy Day each week to discuss and work through this material?

Where will you get together for the first meeting?

What day will everyone need to start going through the *Playbook* (4 days before the first meeting)?

Covenant with other team members to really see this journey through. It's worth doing, but it's worth doing well.

The APEST Ministry Profile Test

We have provided a short *APEST Ministry Profile Test* in the back of the *Playbook.* This test is intended to provide a starting point for discussion; it is not a final assessment.

If you are looking for a more comprehensive in-depth analysis of both individual and group giftings, we suggest you go online at *www.apest.org* and take the *APEST Assessment.* This particular test is designed to give greater clarity and insight to enhance personal and team development.

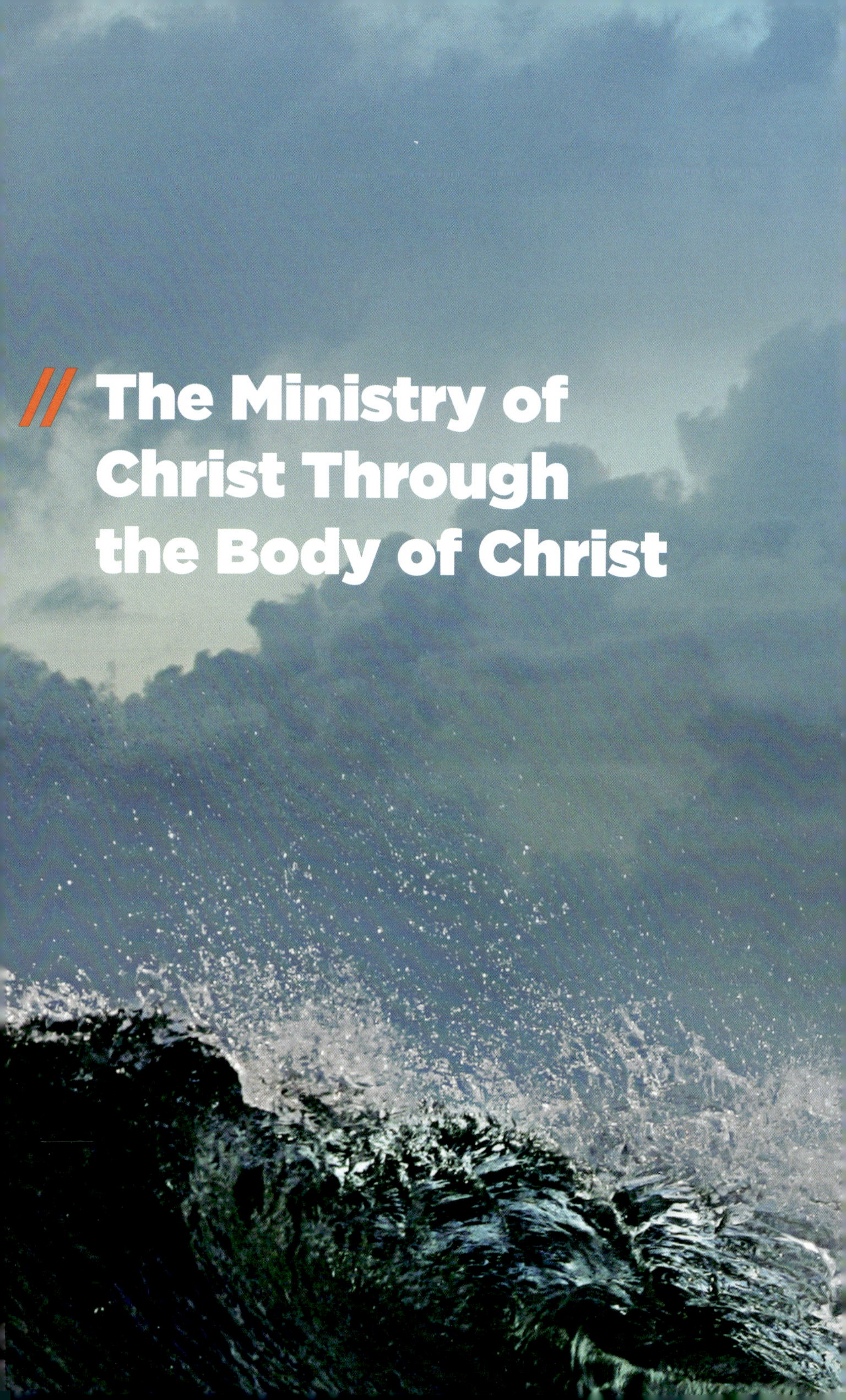

// The Ministry of Christ Through the Body of Christ

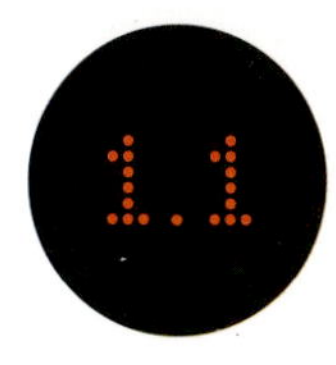

Do you remember the first time you saw a ray of sunlight pass through a prism? It is fascinating how a single beam of light enters one side of the prism and comes out on the other side looking totally different. Where did those new colors come from? Well, all those colors (red, orange, yellow, green, blue, indigo and violet—and everything in between) were actually already inside the ray of light before it passed through the prism. We just couldn't "see" them because they were all so tightly linked together. The cool thing about a prism is that it takes what appears to be a single colored ray of "white" light, separates it and fans it out so we can see the full spectrum of colors "hidden" within it.

With this metaphor in mind, let's take a look at the text in Ephesians 4.

> *But to each one of us grace has been given as Christ apportioned it...So Christ himself gave the apostles, the prophets, the evangelists, the pastors and teachers, to equip his people for works of service, so that the body of Christ may be built up until we all reach unity in the faith and in the knowledge of the Son of God and become mature, attaining to the whole measure of the fullness of Christ.*
>
> *Then we will no longer be infants, tossed back and forth by the waves, and blown here and there by every wind of teaching and by the cunning and craftiness of people in their deceitful scheming. Instead, speaking the truth in love, we will grow to become in every respect the mature body of him who is the head, that is, Christ. From him the whole body, joined and held together by every supporting ligament, grows and builds itself up in love, as each part does its work* (Ephesians 4:7, 11-16).

THE MINISTRY OF CHRIST THROUGH THE BODY OF CHRIST

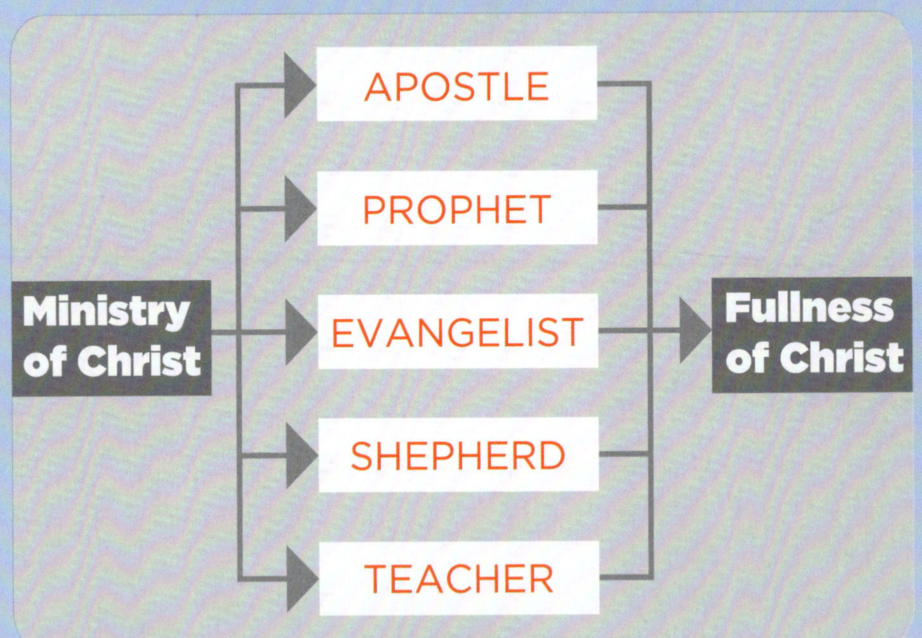

Given the definitions of APEST, we can say with confidence that Jesus was indeed *an apostle, prophet, evangelist, shepherd and teacher.* In fact, he embodies each of these perfectly. He is the embodiment of all five of these functions; they are, in a manner of speaking, "hidden" or concentrated within him. Eugene Peterson notes that the implicit imagery of Ephesians 4 is the ministry of Jesus Christ (APEST) expressing itself through the body of Christ; it prisms out as APEST is distributed among his people. Jesus did this so that his earthly ministry would continue and extend through the body of Christ. If we were to draw it out in a diagram, it would look something like the diagram on the left.

At its core, APEST is about the ministry of Christ working in and through the body of Christ. Taken together, these APEST giftings represent the full spectrum of Christ's ministry. How can we possibly hope to extend the logic and impact of Jesus's ministry if we have less than this five-fold practice of ministry in the church?

Notes

If the APEST giftings originate in the ministry of Christ, then we should expect to be able to observe Jesus functioning in all five of them. Think about the ministry of Christ in the four gospels: Where do you see Jesus described as, or functioning as, an apostle, prophet, evangelist, shepherd or teacher? In the right column, write down the passages or narratives in the gospels where you see Jesus functioning in each of the five APEST ministries. Feel free to review the definitions of the different APEST ministries in the introduction to refresh your memory, or refer to the more in-depth definitions in the table on Day 1.2.

APOSTLE

PROPHET

EVANGELIST

SHEPHERD

TEACHER

Apostle
Easy . . . . Difficult
Prophet
Easy . . . . Difficult
Evangelist
Easy . . . . Difficult
Shepherd
Easy . . . . Difficult
Teacher
Easy . . . . Difficult

Which one of the five APEST ministry roles is easiest for you to associate with Jesus? Which is the most difficult to associate with him? Now try to explain why you responded how you did.

What kind of impression do you think people might have of the church if they only see 2/5ths of Jesus's ministry taking place in and through the church? What will they experience? What will they not experience?

What do you think could happen if the people in your city caught a glimpse of a church that represented the entire spectrum of Christ's ministry contained within APEST? How do you think their view of Christ and his church would change? What would they see? Would there be a sense of awe? What would impact them most?

Every great movement is led by a great leader. Leaders of movements provide the vision and motivation that helps carry the movement forward. Think about the civil rights movement. Dr. Martin Luther King Jr. is undoubtedly one of the greatest leaders to emerge in the history of America. Without his leadership the civil rights movement would not have been able to achieve what it did. His vision for equality and justice, along with his inspirational speeches, gave the civil rights movement the direction and courage it needed to achieve political and social change in America.

"Now is the time to rise from the dark and desolate valley of segregation to the sunlit path of racial justice. Now is the time to lift our nation from the quicksands of racial injustice to the solid rock of brotherhood. Now is the time to make justice a reality for all of God's children." **(Martin Luther King Jr.)**

So what happens when the leader of a movement is removed and is no longer available to provide leadership? How does a movement keep going without its founding leader? Sometimes leaders die, sometimes they are put in prison, or sometimes they just give up. Whatever the reason, they will not always be around to lead the movement. The truth is, if the work of a leader is not carried on through his or her followers or organization, the movement will soon fizzle out and die.

In Ephesians 4:8-10, Paul reminds us that Christ, the revolutionary founder, left his movement and ascended back into the heavens.

He who descended is the very one who ascended higher than all the heavens, in order to fill the whole universe. **(Ephesians 4:10)**

> *So what would happen to the movement Jesus started through his earthly ministry?*
>
> *Would it fizzle out and die?*
>
> *Or would it keep going?*

> It is enough for students to be like their teachers, and servants like their masters. **(Matthew 10:25a)**

In most cases, the leader's absence would have shut the movement down, but Jesus was the smartest leader that has ever lived. In order to make sure his movement would keep going, he did what any good founding leader would do. Before he left the scene, he made sure his followers were able to do the things that he had been doing. By taking his earthly ministry and dividing it into the five basic categories of APEST, Jesus ensured that the full spectrum of his ministry would continue to be represented in the world.

Take a moment to look at the following table of definitions for APEST. Get familiar with them, because they will be helpful for you and your group as you move through the *Playbook* exercises.

APEST Definitions

	APOSTLE	PROPHET	EVANGELIST	SHEPHERD	TEACHER
Core Vocation	custodian of DNA pioneer entrepreneur architect	guardian of the covenant questioner of the status quo	connector to cause recruiter entrepreneur raconteur	discipler humanizer sustainer social integrator	mediator of wisdom & understanding trainer/educator theological formation
Focus	a viable future & expansion of the Christian movement	God-orientation: keeping the movement aligned with God	that people come to know Jesus & join the movement	the community living healthily in the love of the triune God	awareness and integration of truth, especially revealed truth
Spirituality/ Character Complex	adventurous & futuristic has an affinity for systems with an emphasis on risk	transcendent & existential has strong intuition of what is right/ wrong, emphasis on integrity, obedience, & mystery	relational & communal with an emphasis on novelty, sociality, playfulness & celebration	nurturing & communal with an emphasis on healing, wholeness & community	intellectual & philosophical with an emphasis on curiosity, learning, knowledge & the intellect
Leadership Style	decisive design focused strategic	demonstrative motivational	persuasive motivational	inclusive collaborative	prescriptive analytical
Overriding concerns when making decisions	will this help increase our capacity for mission?	will this help us embody God's concerns?	will this help us bring people to a point of conversion?	how will this affect the organization and people in the community?	how does this line up with theology & Scripture?
Contributes to the health of a movement by	ensuring consistency with core ideas (DNA); laying new foundations & architecting systems around mobilization & extension	anchoring the movement in God's values; providing critical feedback for constant realignment	explicitly valuing the gospel as our core story; adding new people; sharing the message in the local vernacular	cultivating and integrating people into a socially cohesive community that fosters relational health	systematizing and articulating the multi-dimensional aspects of truth; optimizing operational efficiency
Short-fallings	driven, demanding, insensitive to people	ideological and demanding, short-sighted, simplistic	anything to "make the deal," not demanding enough	obsessive need for harmony, aversion to risk	demand for ideology conformity, lack of urgency
Historical Examples	Jesus, Paul, Peter, Patrick, John Wesley, Aimee Semple McPherson	Jesus, Jeremiah, James, St. Benedict, Martin Luther, Bonhoeffer, Martin Luther King Jr.	Jesus, Phillip, George Whitfield, Billy Graham, Rick Warren	Jesus, St. Francis, Jean Vanier, Mother Teresa , Eugene Peterson	Jesus, Apollos, Augustine, Aquinas, John Calvin, Henri Nouwen

COACHING MOMENT

Paul prayed earlier in Ephesians that we would be strengthened through the Holy Spirit. While the ministries of APEST are at the very center of how Paul sees the ministry in the church, it is only through the empowering presence of the Spirit that we find the strength to express our respective APEST ministries and extend Christ's ministry in and through the church.

Through APEST, the church has been given the same potential for revolutionary impact that Jesus demonstrated through his ministry. The degree to which we are able to activate these giftings and unleash them will be the degree to which we are able to become a permanent revolution once again.

Notes

Think about the ministry of Christ and list some of the reasons why you think his ministry had such a revolutionary impact. After you list those things, try to identify which APEST category of ministry Jesus was demonstrating through that part of his ministry.

Example Reason: He taught people with authority and not like the religious leaders of his day
Example APEST Catagory: Teacher

Reason Why Jesus's Ministry Was Revolutionary	Possible APEST Gifting

The basic rule of thumb is that if we do what Christ did, then we will reap the fruit that Christ reaped. He promises as much and more (John 15:16, Ephesians 3:20). Through the ministries of APEST, we are equipped for the same revolutionary impact Jesus demonstrated in his ministry.

> Now to him who is able to do immeasurably more than all we ask or imagine, according to his power that is at work within us... **(Ephesians 3:20)**

Do you believe the church can have a revolutionary impact on society and culture? How about your city? What might that look like?

The fact that Jesus gave these gifts to the church to continue the revolution that he started is quite challenging. How does it make you feel that you have been gifted by Christ to help continue the revolution?

These giftings, as mentioned before, are not just given to leaders. They are given "to each one of us." How does this change the way you see your role in the body of Christ?

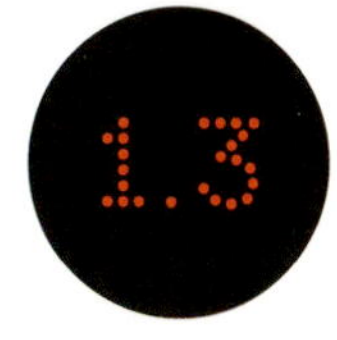

When going through a study like this, we can easily dismiss words like "movement" and "revolutionary" as being idealistic or out of touch with reality. We as the authors are not using these words just for shock value. Jesus Christ really did start a revolutionary movement that began with about 120 people on the margins of society and saturated over half the Roman Empire in less than 300 years.

And when they could not find them, they dragged Jason and some of the brothers before the city authorities, shouting, "These men **who have turned the world upside down** have come here also... **(Acts 17:6 ESV)**

Even after the revolutionary founder was physically removed, the revolution kept growing exponentially from generation to generation. A movement that demonstrates this kind of ongoing influence on culture and society definitely qualifies as revolutionary. The first 300 years of church history reveal that Jesus originally designed the church to be a transformative, continuous, people-focused movement (Ephesians 3:20-21).

Ephesians 4 makes a pretty bold claim on our lives and churches. It calls us to broaden our imaginations and open ourselves up to recognizing not only the full spectrum of Christ's ministry in the church today, but also the full potential within the body of Christ to be a permanent revolution once again. Christ designed us, the church, to be a living organism that experiences continuous movement from generation to generation. In order for this to happen, we have to face up to two things.

First, we are called to really believe and live into what God has built into the church. Do we really believe that Christ has given the church everything it needs in order to be a permanent revolution? In order to get to the pattern of Christ's ministry in Ephesians 4:7-16, we first have to wrestle with the promise of God's power in Ephesians 3:20-21.

But when you ask, you must believe and not doubt, because the one who doubts is like a wave of the sea, blown and tossed by the wind. **(James 1:6)**

COACHING MOMENT

James says that a doubting person is double-minded. This person says one thing but actually believes something else. Persistent doubt makes us unstable and vulnerable to the forces of the enemy. Bringing your thoughts into alignment with what the word of God says is the first challenge facing you as a leader. Why have you not lived out what Ephesians 3:20-21 is clearly referring to? What makes you resistant to its claims? Do an audit of your thinking about APEST and articulate what you believe, and why you have believed it thus far.

Rather, speaking the truth in love, we are to grow up in every way into him who is the head, into Christ, from whom the whole body, joined and held together by every joint with which it is equipped, when each part is working properly, makes the body grow so that it builds itself up in love. **(Ephesians 4:15-16 ESV)**

Second, we need to change the way we see ministry and leadership in the church. This Ephesian letter was not written to a group of leaders, but to average people in the church. The text says that "each one of us has been given grace according to the measure of Christ's gift." These APEST giftings are not given to *some* people in the church so they can train and equip *other* people to do works of ministry. Rather, the text is *all about* body ministry (vs. 12-16) as APEST has been given to ***each one of us.***

Paul continues this inclusive language in Ephesians 4:8 when he says that these gifts were given to "men." The literal word is *anthropos*, which means human beings as a whole (including both men and women). So from the very beginning, Paul is "ordaining" the entire body of Christ into the work of ministry. Add to this the truth that the recipients of this letter included slaves, women and people of different races (Ephesians 2:11ff, Ephesians 5). These were ordinary people, not a group of ordained leaders.

This is revolutionary language because it enlists the entire body of Christ in the revolution that Jesus started. Ephesians 4 is about *everyone having a ministry,* not just a few people being the ministers! We all have been given a measure of grace to extend the ministry of Christ to those around us. There are no spectators. Everyone gets to play.

In addition, in order to live up to this high calling of being a permanent revolution, we will need more than just two out of the five ministries to operate. Like a basketball team, we need all five players on the court if we are going to be able to press back against the forces of the enemy and become the fullness of Christ in the world. Without all five ministries operating in the church, we will not be able to mature or be the permanent revolution we were designed to be. With this in mind, reread Ephesians 4:7-16 and answer the questions on the next page.

Now to him who is able to do far more abundantly than all that we ask or think, according to the power at work within us, to him be glory in the church and in Christ Jesus throughout all generations, forever and ever. Amen. **(Ephesians 3:20-21 ESV)**

When God raised Jesus from the dead, he proved that no obstacle was too small for him. Do you believe God can do more than you could possibly ask or imagine?

Why do you think we struggle to believe this?

If God were to use your team to start a permanent revolution in your city, what do you think it would look like? Describe some of the things that would be different if your church had a revolutionary impact in your city.

Why is it important to recognize that the APEST giftings have been given to the entire body of Christ and not just a group of leaders?

As someone who is (or will be) leading a team, how should your understanding that everyone has been gifted by Christ for ministry affect the way you lead and do ministry?

Most likely, no one is completely familiar with every kind of ministry represented in APEST. Which ones would you like to become more familiar with, and why?

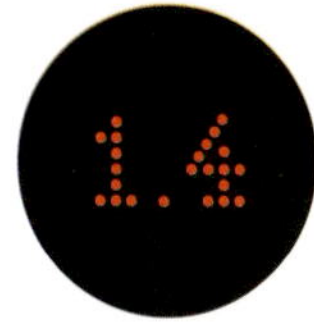

All this sounds great, but do we really believe it?

Paul tells us in Romans 10:17 that faith comes by hearing, and hearing by the word of God. Today's action step is really simple. We want you to memorize Ephesians 3:20-21. The process of internalizing Scripture allows our minds to be re-ordered around God's reality. Think of it like eating; the food you eat during a meal continues to affect your body long after the meal itself is over. Internalization of Scripture is a bit like this: God's word will continue to work in you long after you've memorized it, renewing your mind, shaping your desires, guiding your thought life and building your faith. It's how we go from knowing the information of God's word to really digesting God's word, getting it "into" us so it can do what it's designed to do.

As you memorize this passage, ask God to do amazing things in and through you.

> *Now to him who is able to do immeasurably more than all we ask or imagine, according to his power that is at work within us, to him be glory in the church and in Christ Jesus throughout all generations, forever and ever! Amen*

So then faith comes by hearing, and hearing by the word of God.
(Romans 10:17 NKJV)

Do not be conformed to this world, but be transformed by the renewal of your mind, that by testing you may discern what is the will of God, what is good and acceptable and perfect.
(Romans 12:2 ESV)

Your commandment makes me wiser than my enemies, for it is ever with me.
I have more understanding than all my teachers, for your testimonies are my meditation.
I understand more than the aged, for I keep your precepts.
(Psalm 119:98-100 ESV)

SYNERGY // The Ministry of Christ Through the Body of Christ

Therefore let us pursue the things which make for peace and the things by which one may edify another.
(Romans 14:19) NKJV

After your group gets done hanging out and socializing, start your meeting with this time of encouragement: Since each one of us has been gifted by Christ to represent a portion of his ministry, talk about how you have seen the ministry of Jesus show up through your team members. This is a time of positive encouragement where you can say how you have seen Jesus express his ministry through the different people in your group. Give specific examples when possible.

> *On the first day (1.1), we looked at how the ministry of Christ is broken up into the five basic categories of APEST. Discuss with the group how you answered this question: Which one of the five APEST ministry roles is easiest for you to associate with Jesus? Which one is the most difficult to associate with him? Why?*
>
> *On day two (1.2), we talked about how the APEST giftings were given to each one of us so that we could continue the revolution that Jesus started. Discuss in your group the idea of the church being a revolutionary presence in the world. What would this look like in your city?*
>
> *On day three (1.3) we talked about the need to believe in the power of God to do even more than we ask or imagine. Discuss how our faith in God's power is directly linked to our call to be a permanent revolution.*

On day four (1.4), we asked you to memorize Ephesians 3:20-21. Ask those who did memorize it to talk about how this verse has impacted them.

End your meeting with a prayer thanking God for the way he has uniquely gifted each one of us to serve and represent Christ to those around us. As you pray, call out each gift that the Holy Spirit has given to your group. Naming each gift and connecting them with their bearers can deepen our appreciation of how God uniquely equips the body.

Now to him who is able to do far more abundantly than all that we ask or think, according to the power at work within us, to him be glory in the church and in Christ Jesus throughout all generations, forever and ever. Amen. **(Ephesians 3:20-21 ESV)**

1.6

CALIBRATION // The Ministry of Christ Through the Body of Christ

I do not ask that you take them out of the world, but that you keep them from the evil one. They are not of the world, just as I am not of the world. Sanctify them in the truth; your word is truth. As you sent me into the world, so I have sent them into the world. And for their sake I consecrate myself, that they also may be sanctified in truth. "I do not ask for these only, but also for those who will believe in me through their word, that they may all be one, just as you, Father, are in me, and I in you, that they also may be in us, so that the world may believe that you have sent me. **(John 17:15-21 ESV)**

Hopefully this study is shedding new light on how the original, revolutionary ministry of Christ can continue in our day. We are designed for permanent revolution because the very ministry of Christ has been separated into five categories and given to *each one of us.* The ministry of Christ now takes place through the body of Christ.

If the church is going to be a permanent revolution once again, it will have to start with our faith in God's power to work through *each one of us.* The same revolution that took place through the ministry of Christ can take place through the body of Christ. We are a permanent revolution waiting to happen.

The question is, then, what primary ministry has Jesus called you to? Are you willing to embrace it and learn more about it?

When we open ourselves to God and let him use us as the body of Christ, the work he does through us will not look the same for everyone. Some are gifted as apostles and will do apostolic kinds of things. Some are gifted as prophets and will do prophetic things. Some are gifted as evangelists and will do evangelistic things. Others are gifted as shepherds and will do what shepherds do best. Still others are gifted as teachers and will do what teachers do best.

No one person can fully represent the entirety of Christ's ministry. We need all five APEST ministries in order to represent the fullness of Christ's ministry.

So are we willing to open the door and recognize the full spectrum of Christ's ministry in the body, or will we continue to settle for a two-fold understanding of ministry and leadership in the church?

This week we have been looking at how the ministry of Christ is carried out through the body of Christ. Look at Ephesians 4:13 again: *"Until we all reach unity in the faith and in the knowledge of the Son of God and become mature, attaining to the whole measure of the fullness of Christ."* All of us are meant to express a particular shade of color within the spectrum of Christ's ministry. When the five giftings come together and work as a body, the church and the world are exposed to the full spectrum of Christ's ministry in all its beautiful shades and colors.

Consider praying this prayer as a way of thanking Christ for giving you the opportunity to be an expression of his grace in the world:

> *Christ, I open myself up to you as the giver of many gifts. Thank you for giving me a measure of grace to represent you in the world. Help me to see myself and those on my team as reflections of your glory. Lead us into a full expression of your ministry. Start a revolution...again.*

I thank my God in all my remembrance of you, always in every prayer of mine for you all making my prayer with joy, because of your partnership in the gospel from the first day until now. And I am sure of this, that he who began a good work in you will bring it to completion at the day of Jesus Christ. **(Philippians 1:3-6 ESV)**

The Order of Creation, The Order of Redemption

A few verses in Ephesians 4 often get overlooked. At first glance they seem, well, out of place. Why all this talk about Christ descending and ascending? What does "leading captivity captive" mean? And what does it have to do with APEST? Is Paul getting off topic here, or is there something in vs. 8-10 worth paying attention to? Let's take a look.

> I, therefore, the prisoner of the Lord, beseech you to walk worthy of the calling with which you were called, with all lowliness and gentleness, with longsuffering, bearing with one another in love, endeavoring to keep the unity of the Spirit in the bond of peace. There is one body and one Spirit, just as you were called in one hope of your calling; one Lord, one faith, one baptism; one God and Father of all, who is above all, and through all, and in you all. But to each one of us grace was given according to the measure of Christ's gift. Therefore he says: "When he ascended on high, he led captivity captive, and gave gifts to men." (Now this, "he ascended"—what does it mean but that he also first descended into the lower parts of the earth? He who descended is also the One who ascended far above all the heavens, that he might fill all things.)
> **(Ephesians 4:1-10 NKJV)**

When Paul says Christ descended, he is referring to the incarnation. God became a human being. This, in and of itself, is worth looking into. But Paul is actually wanting to us to pay attention not to what happened at the beginning, but at the very end. When Jesus left the earth and ascended to the right hand of God, two important things took place.

He led captivity captive

The word "captivity" actually appears twice, back to back, in the original text of Ephesians. This seemingly pointless repetition begs the question: Why mention the same word twice?

The answer is found in the way Christ is being portrayed. In this passage, Christ is pictured as a liberator who enters into battle, takes his enemies captive, and parades them through the city as a public display of his victory. Paul repeats himself to emphasize the all-encompassing nature of Christ's liberating work. Christ sets us free from captivity and he also takes the very thing that was holding us bondage into captivity. It is freedom at every level.

He gave gifts (APEST)

These gifts are not offices or leadership positions. They are people who, having been set free, are given the opportunity to represent the ministry of Christ as his beloved and redeemed apostles, prophets, evangelists, shepherds and teachers. This opportunity to represent Christ through APEST is a grace given to each one of us.

These two things are uniquely tied together. It is the liberating work of Christ that allows people to be apostles, prophets, evangelists, shepherds and teachers. APEST is what emerges when people are in Christ. So in a sense, Ephesians 4 is simply giving us the language to describe how people will function in the body once they have been set free by the gospel.

The order of creation, the order of redemption

Because APEST flows directly out of the liberating work of Christ, we think APEST is found not only in the order of redemption (the church) but also in what theologians call the order of creation (general humanity). In other words, APEST people can be observed outside of the church, not just inside the church. We suggest the unique capacities associated with each APEST gifting can actually to be traced back to how we are designed as human beings. Paul alludes to this very idea in Ephesians 2:8-10:

> *For it is by grace you have been saved, through faith—and this is not from yourselves, it is the gift of God—not by works, so that no one can boast. For we are God's handiwork, created in Christ Jesus to do good works, which God prepared in advance for us to do.*

You made all the delicate, inner parts of my body and knit me together in my mother's womb. Thank you for making me so wonderfully complex! Your workmanship is marvelous—how well I know it. **(Psalm 139:13-14 NLT)**

COACHING MOMENT

Ephesians 2:8-10 is actually a smaller, more condensed version of Ephesians 4:7-12. In both passages, it is the work of Christ that releases us to be who God has originally designed us to be. The good works mentioned in chapter 2, which were prepared beforehand for us to do, are expressed through the work of ministry that flows out of APEST in chapter 4. This makes sense given the image in Ephesians 4 of Christ as a liberator. He takes what is already present within us and redeems it, realigning it for his own purposes, giving it new direction and significance.

These APEST giftings are given to us by the God-Man, Jesus Christ. So right from the beginning we are alerted to the divine, yet equally human, origin of these gifts. It should not surprise us, then, to see APEST represented in the common experience of what it means to be a human being.

This is one of the reasons why we see APEST as being lifelong callings. They originate in the order of creation and continue to express themselves in the church through the five-fold ministries of APEST. As Andrew Dowesett says, "Being an apostle, a prophet, an evangelist, a shepherd or a teacher is not something we become at the point of liberation. Rather, it is who we are from the beginning." This has huge implications for developing God's people for engagement and ministry not only inside the church, but also outside of it.

Notes

Before we move on, let's pause for a moment and ask a few simple questions:

What are the "gifts" that Jesus gives when he returns from battle? (vs. 8-11)

Why are these "gifts" given to the body of Christ? (vs. 12)

This will continue until we all come to such unity in our faith and knowledge of God's Son that we will be mature in the Lord, measuring up to the full and complete standard of Christ. Then we will no longer be immature like children. We won't be tossed and blown about by every wind of new teaching. We will not be influenced when people try to trick us with lies so clever they sound like the truth. Instead, we will speak the truth in love, growing in every way more and more like Christ, who is the head of his body, the church. He makes the whole body fit together perfectly. As each part does its own special work, it helps the other parts grow, so that the whole body is healthy and growing and full of love. **(Ephesians 4:13-16 NLT)**

What happens as a result of the equipping that takes place through each of the APEST ministries? (vs. 13-16) Think about some of the people you know (past or present) who are not in Christ. Using the descriptions above, how do you see APEST reflected in their lives? List their names and which APEST category seems to be most evident in their lives. Try to think of someone for each APEST category.

Name:

Most evident APEST category:

Name:

Most evident APEST category:

Name:

Most evident APEST category:

Name:

Most evident APEST category:

Name:

Most evident APEST category:

Ephesians 4:8-10 portrays Christ as a liberator. In order to appreciate what Paul is saying and how this relates to APEST, we have to look at this passage more closely. In it, Paul is actually quoting Psalm 68:18. Let's take a look at that psalm.

> *The chariots of God are tens of thousands and thousands of thousands; the Lord has come from Sinai into his sanctuary. When you ascended on high, you took many captives; you received gifts from people, even from the rebellious—that you, LORD God, might dwell there. Praise be to the Lord, to God our Savior, who daily bears our burdens. Our God is a God who saves; from the Sovereign LORD comes escape from death. (Psalm 68:17-20)*

In King David's era, when a warrior returned from battle as a victor, they celebrated their victory by marching through the city in a parade of sorts. The captives taken in battle would often follow behind the victor in this parade as a way of visualizing the victory. The parade started at the edge of town and moved toward the king's palace, where the warrior would receive gifts for his valiant efforts. So it looked something like this:

Psalm 68:18

DESCENDED **ASCENDED**

Led captivity captive and received gifts

Victorious Battle

Who is this King of glory?
The LORD strong and mighty,
the LORD mighty in battle!
(Psalm 24:8)

David is using this imagery of the victorious warrior returning from battle and applying it to God as the liberator of Israel. God is pictured as descending from Mount Sinai, entering into battle, liberating his people from slavery, and later ascending to Mount Zion (Jerusalem), where he receives gifts from his people.

I also pray that you will understand the incredible greatness of God's power for us who believe him. This is the same mighty power that raised Christ from the dead and seated him in the place of honor at God's right hand in the heavenly realms. Now he is far above any ruler or authority or power or leader or anything else—not only in this world but also in the world to come. God has put all things under the authority of Christ and has made him head over all things for the benefit of the church. And the church is his body; it is made full and complete by Christ, who fills all things everywhere with himself. **(Ephesians 1:19-23 NLT)**

Now back to Ephesians. Paul is saying that what took place through the exodus and God's subsequent enthronement in Jerusalem is very similar to what took place through the work of Christ—with one exception. Christ also descended into battle, led captivity captive and ascended to a throne. However, instead of receiving gifts at his ascension, Christ actually gives gifts! It looks something like this:

Ephesians 4:8-10

DESCENDED **ASCENDED**

Led captivity captive and GAVE gifts

Victorious Battle

These APEST giftings are not arbitrary. They emerge directly out of the cosmic battle between Christ and the enslaving powers of darkness. Through our newfound freedom in Christ, we are given the opportunity to represent his ministry through the five-fold expressions of apostles, prophets, evangelists, shepherds and teachers.

COACHING MOMENT

In Ephesians 3:1-9 Paul zooms in to give us an up-close snapshot of how he received his apostleship. Paul understood this calling to be a gift of grace. Paul knew his apostleship was definitely unique, but he also knew that he was not the only one who received grace for ministry. In Ephesians 4:7, Paul zooms out to acknowledge that "to each one of us grace has been given according to the measure of Christ's gift." It's almost as if Paul was saying, "Yes, I received my apostleship as a gift of grace, and this is unique in the greater scope of God's plan. But I am not the only one who has received grace for ministry. Each one of us has received grace according to the measure of Christ's gift. He gave some to be apostles, some prophets, some evangelists, some shepherds, some teachers."

Notes

The opportunity for us to live into our unique APEST callings is possible because Christ was willing to descend into battle; wage war with the principalities, powers and the rulers of darkness (6:12); and set us free.

How does it make you feel to know that your APEST gifting is something that was secured for you in a cosmic battle?

> Although I am less than the least of all the Lord's people, this grace was given me: to preach to the Gentiles the boundless riches of Christ. [Ephesians 3:8]
>
> *In this passage, Paul says that the opportunity to preach Christ among the Gentiles was a "grace" that was given to him. Even though Paul's apostleship was unique (see previous Coaching Moment), he recognized that he was not the only one who had received "grace" for ministry. Paul said, "each one of us has received grace according to the measure of Christ's gift." Why is the opportunity to represent the ministry of Christ through APEST considered a "gift of grace"?*

One of the challenges we all face as human beings is coming to terms with who we were created to be. All of us are uniquely designed by God. We are created in his image. This means all the beauty and complexity of who God is, and what he does, is somehow reflected in each one of us.

Are there areas of your gifting that have become points of tension between you and God? Do you feel he should have given you a greater measure of gifting, or a different kind of gifting all together? Is it possible to release that disappointment and offer yourself to him as an act of worship?

This reflection is undoubtedly marred and distorted by sin, but even our sin does not completely erase his image within us. In Christ this image is renewed, and it comes more clearly into focus. (Ephesians 4:17-24) As reflections, we do not get to choose what we "look" like. It's not something we can pick and choose, as if we were shopping at the store. In terms of how we are designed for ministry, we can only be who we are. No more, no less.

Coming to terms with this truth can be difficult. We can easily find ourselves saying things like:

But by the grace of God I am what I am, and his grace to me was not without effect. **(1 Corinthians 15:10a)**

"If only I had her ability to ________, I would be so much more ________."

"If only I could be more like ________. Then I could have ________."

I appeal to you, brothers and sisters, in the name of our Lord Jesus Christ, that all of you agree with one another in what you say and that there be no divisions among you, but that you be perfectly united in mind and thought. **(1 Corinthians 1:10)**

COACHING MOMENT

In Ephesians chapters 1-3, Paul unpacks our spiritual identity—who we are in Christ. In Ephesians 4, Paul moves on to talk about our vocational identity—who we are in the body of Christ. It is important to keep these two identities in proper perspective. You can always tell when you are allowing your vocational identity to take center stage. Insecurity, envy, competition and shame will begin to define your ministry experience.

This kind of thinking often leads us to ignore, even despise, our own gifting. Left untended, this mentality will produce envy and jealousy, the very things that undermine a group's ability to function as a team.

The solution is not to ignore the value of other people's gifting. This would lead to a different kind of problem. The solution is found in recognizing the grace that has been distributed to each and every one of us. We are all unique gifts that Christ is giving to the body. Paul says it like this:

For we are God's handiwork, created in Christ Jesus to do good works, which God prepared in advance for us to do. (Ephesians 2:10)

Woe to him who strives with him who formed him, a pot among earthen pots! Does the clay say to him who forms it, 'What are you making?' or 'Your work has no handles'? **(Isaiah 45:9 ESV)**

When Paul says that we are his workmanship, he is using a word that was often translated in other writings as a "work of art." Whether it's a poem, a sculpture, a song, a painting or even a "killer app" on a smartphone, Paul says that in Christ we have been uniquely shaped and crafted for ministry.

Notes

Have you ever thought about receiving yourself as a gift? If so, in what way?

If not, why not?

How satisfied are you with the way God has gifted you for ministry?

What has led you to be this way?

The five-fold giftings of APEST are given as a result of Christ's victory in battle. If we refuse to accept the way we have been gifted as apostles, prophets, evangelists, shepherds and teachers, what are we essentially saying about Christ's efforts in battle?

About ourselves?

ACTION // The Order of Creation, the Order of Redemption

APOSTLE

PROPHET

EVANGELIST

SHEPHERD

TEACHER

Take a moment to review the definitions of APEST provided in this *Playbook* on Day 1.2. With these definitions in mind, think about each person on your team. Which APEST ministries are most evident to you in this season of their lives?

Go with your first impression, acknowledging that your team discussion tomorrow may change your opinion. Fill out the following table and be prepared to share it tomorrow with your group.

Name:

APEST Category Most Evident To You:

Name:

APEST Category Most Evident To You:

Name:

APEST Category Most Evident To You:

Name:

APEST Category Most Evident To You:

Name:

APEST Category Most Evident To You:

Name:

APEST Category Most Evident To You:

Name:

APEST Category Most Evident To You:

Name:

APEST Category Most Evident To You:

For no good tree bears bad fruit, nor again does a bad tree bear good fruit, for each tree is known by its own fruit. For figs are not gathered from thornbushes, nor are grapes picked from a bramble bush. The good person out of the good treasure of his heart produces good, and the evil person out of his evil treasure produces evil, for out of the abundance of the heart his mouth speaks. **(Luke 6:43-45 ESV)**

Each one of your team members is a gift. Take a moment to thank God for each one of them, giving special attention to how each one adds value to the team. After you have given thanks for each team member, briefly write down why each team member is valuable to the team. Be specific. You will be asked to share this tomorrow with your team.

I thank my God always when I remember you in my prayers, because I hear of your love and of the faith that you have toward the Lord Jesus and for all the saints, and I pray that the sharing of your faith may become effective for the full knowledge of every good thing that is in us for the sake of Christ. **(Philemon 1:4-6 ESV)**

Name:

Value to the team:

Name:

Value to the team:

Name:

Value to the team:

Name:

Value to the team:

Name:

Value to the team:

Name:

Value to the team:

Name:

Value to the team:

Name:

Value to the team:

I give thanks to my God always for you because of the grace of God that was given you in Christ Jesus, that in every way you were enriched in him in all speech and all knowledge— even as the testimony about Christ was confirmed among you— so that you are not lacking in any gift, as you wait for the revealing of our Lord Jesus Christ, who will sustain you to the end, guiltless in the day of our Lord Jesus Christ. God is faithful, by whom you were called into the fellowship of his Son, Jesus Christ our Lord.
(1 Corinthians 1:4-9 ESV)

SYNERGY // The Order of Creation, the Order of Redemption

Today we will be sharing the insights you have gained through our study of Ephesians 4:7-11. Here are some questions to get the conversations going:

On day one (2.1), we looked at how the APEST giftings flow directly out of the liberating work of Christ. This helps us make sense of why we see APEST functioning in both Christians and non-Christians. They are present in the orders of creation as well as the orders of redemption. How does this change the way you see these giftings and what they are about?

On day two (2.2), you were asked this question: The opportunity for us to live into our unique APEST callings is made possible because Christ was willing to descend into battle; wage war with the principalities, powers and the rulers of darkness (6:12); and set us free. How does it make you feel to know that your APEST gifting is something that was secured for you in a cosmic battle? Share your answer with the group.

In one of the coaching moments on day three (2.3), we talked about how our vocational identity in APEST should flow out of our common spiritual identity in Christ. Why is it important to make sure our spiritual identity serves as the foundation for our vocational identity and not the other way around?

In other words, what happens when our vocational identity in APEST becomes more important than our spiritual identity in Christ?

Now you get to share how you see APEST functioning in your team. Flip to day four (2.4) and share with the rest of the group how you filled out the two tables in the notes section. Before you do this, make sure to read the coaching moment.

COACHING MOMENT

A word of caution here: This is merely an exercise to help you start processing your team through the lens of APEST. Do not come to any conclusions about yourself or your teammates too quickly. Discerning our vocational identities is often a process of discovery that happens over time. It requires experimentation and continuous feedback from those who know us best. So it is best to frame your observations about yourself and your teammates with more subjective language like, "I feel like my primary APEST gifting might be..." or, "I could be wrong, but you come across to me as a __________." Most of all, allow people the freedom to agree or disagree with your observation.

After you finish sharing how you see APEST functioning in your team and how each person adds value to it, select one person on the team to end your time together with a prayer of thanksgiving for each person on your team.

We always thank God, the Father of our Lord Jesus Christ, when we pray for you, because we have heard of your faith in Christ Jesus and of the love you have for all God's people—the faith and love that spring from the hope stored up for you in heaven and about which you have already heard in the true message of the gospel.
(Colossians 1:3-5)

CALIBRATION // The Order of Creation, the Order of Redemption

We took a pretty deep dive into Ephesians 4:7-11 this week. This passage of Scripture, while often overlooked, is jam-packed with meaningful insights about how APEST flows directly out of the liberating work of Christ. Recognizing this connection helps us crack the code, as it were, to what these five ministries are really about.

Apostles tend to be strategic, like to pioneer projects and bring design and systems thinking to bear. In the created orders, apostles might well be people who start a business rather than work in an established one, or consultants who diagnose problems and prescribe innovative solutions. In short, they are architects of innovation and have a natural inclination toward exploration and adventure.

Prophets tend to see the world from an alternative perspective, which is why the creative arts often function as a commons for people with prophetic sensibilities. Sensitive to alternate ways of seeing the world, they often question the status quo. They often have a concern for issues related to justice and societal reform, which can express itself in social, political or environmental activism.

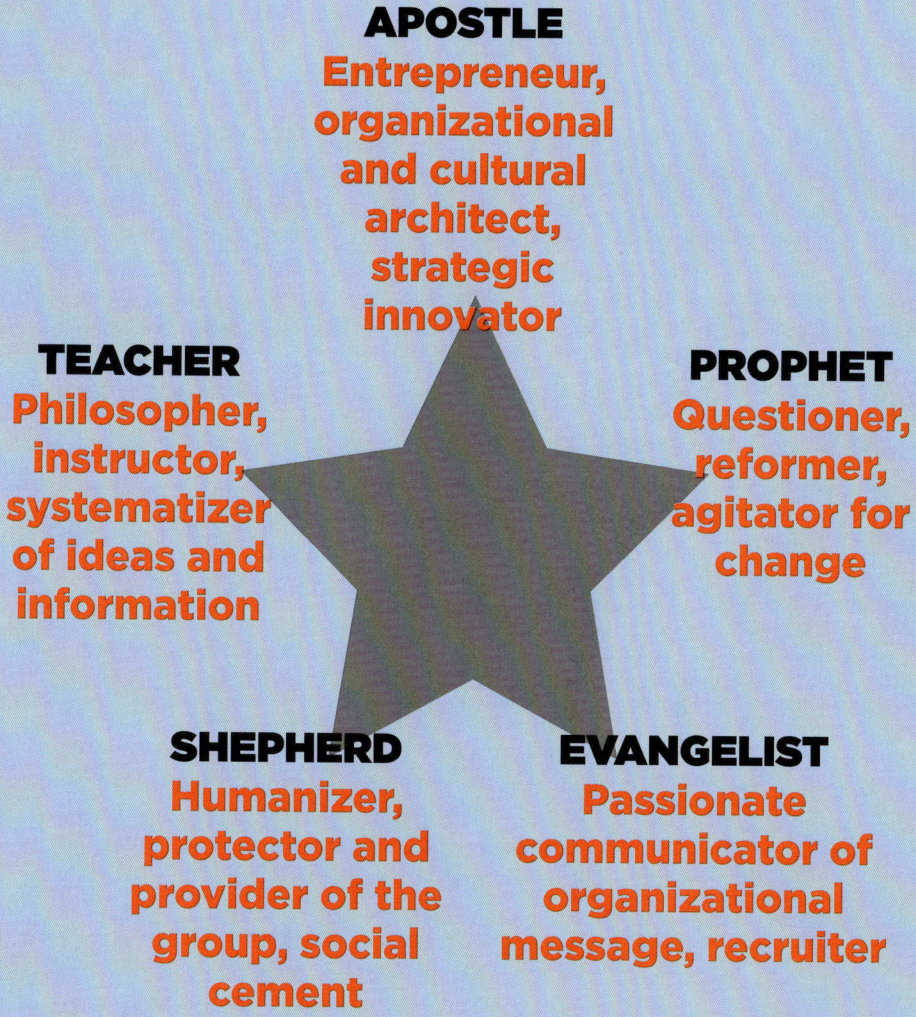

APOSTLE
Entrepreneur, organizational and cultural architect, strategic innovator

TEACHER
Philosopher, instructor, systematizer of ideas and information

PROPHET
Questioner, reformer, agitator for change

SHEPHERD
Humanizer, protector and provider of the group, social cement

EVANGELIST
Passionate communicator of organizational message, recruiter

Then Philip began with that very passage of Scripture and told him the good news about Jesus. **(Acts 8:35)**

Evangelists tend to be passionate communicators of ideas and values. If something is important to them, you will hear about it in a compelling, persuasive way. Like the apostolic type, they tend to be somewhat go-get-'em and entrepreneurial, yet in a different sort of way. As opposed to being designers of systems, they tend to be influencers of people. They can see the potential for good in almost any person, place or thing. This natural optimism allows them to see opportunities for new and meaningful relationships at every turn. As the saying goes, they never meet a stranger. This makes them great recruiters for any organization or movement. Like it or not, they often demonstrate the qualities of a good salesperson, which is why they are naturally drawn to jobs that allow them to engage in promoting products and services through marketing, fundraising and recruiting personnel.

Shepherds tend to find great fulfillment in taking care of people, looking after their needs and making sure the group stays healthy and connected. This can express itself through affirming, nurturing relationships, or by closely supervising operations to ensure resources are adequately managed and distributed within the group. This impulse to meet the social and operational needs of the group allows the group to reach a level of sustainability it otherwise would not. Shepherds are often found in the vocational fields of counseling, human resources and caretaker industries, which can include law enforcement. They humanize the organization by making sure we pay attention to the "people factor."

Teachers are primarily concerned with helping people learn. They tend to be philosophical, thoughtful and intellectual miners who are constantly pursuing new information, or rearranging existing information into new patterns of meaning. They can also be natural trainers, with a penchant for developing curriculum and learning processes to help people learn how to perform various kinds of tasks. Being keenly aware of how ideas shape human life, they naturally inspire a love of wisdom and understanding. They are often found working in educational settings as well as companies and organizations that specialize in archiving, managing and producing information.

There's no doubt these kinds of people are already present within society—as we've said, they are built into the very orders of creation. And like all of creation, each one of them reaches their intended purpose in Christ by expressing themselves in and through the church for the glory of God. (Ephesians 3:20-21)

This way of seeing APEST fits well with what we know about Christ and his redeeming work for us. He takes ordinary people, sets them free and gives them as gifts, in the form of APEST, to the body of Christ. Not only do we find our spiritual identity in Christ, through APEST we are given our vocational identity as well. This opportunity to represent the ministry of Christ in and the through the church is a gift of grace. Our challenge is to receive ourselves, and one another, for what we truly are: a work of art, uniquely shaped for his eternal purpose.

Notes

If you had to narrow it down, what would be the most valuable thing you have learned this week...

from Ephesians?

about yourself?

about your team?

Out of these three things, which one seems to be the most helpful for you at this time? Why?

RECREATE // The Order of Creation, the Order of Redemption

I (Tim) can remember the first time I went into the Smithsonian art museum. I was in seventh grade, and it was my first field trip out of town. Thinking back, art was the furthest thing from my mind. I was just glad to get out of the classroom. The entire trip is pretty much a haze. I don't remember much about it.

The one thing I do remember is the trip back to school. I was staring out the bus window thinking about all the things I saw in the museum that day. I remember thinking to myself, "How is a big red ball with white paint running down the middle of it considered art?" In fact, I saw a lot of things that day that made me wonder, "How is this art? I could make that in my front yard!" Needless to say, my appreciation for what rightly can be called "art" has grown since then.

For you formed my inward parts; you knitted me together in my mother's womb. I praise you, for I am fearfully and wonderfully made. Wonderful are your works; my soul knows it very well. My frame was not hidden from you, when I was being made in secret, intricately woven in the depths of the earth. Your eyes saw my unformed substance; in your book were written, every one of them, the days that were formed for me, when as yet there was none of them.
(Psalm 139:13–16 ESV)

Think about Ephesians 2:10: "For we are God's handiwork, created in Christ Jesus to do good works, which God prepared in advance for us to do." When Paul says that we are his handiwork in Ephesians 2:10, he is saying that we are a uniquely crafted work of art. And just as art evokes different responses in people, we can expect to have different responses to ourselves and to one another. The important thing is to remember is that we, individually and as a group, are a collection of God's workmanship. Not everyone may see you this way. You may not see yourself this way. It doesn't change the truth of who you are. God has put you on display as a work of art in the body of Christ.

Spend some time thanking God for making you and your team as a work of art. Consider praying this prayer:

God, thank you for setting me free to be who you have designed me to be. You are the great liberator! Forgive me for not receiving myself as a gift from you. Forgive me for not receiving the people on my team as a gift from you. Open my eyes to the beauty of your work within me and my team. By the power of your Spirit and the energy in your grace, move us deeper into our callings. Equip us for the challenges at hand.

// Personal APEST Profiles

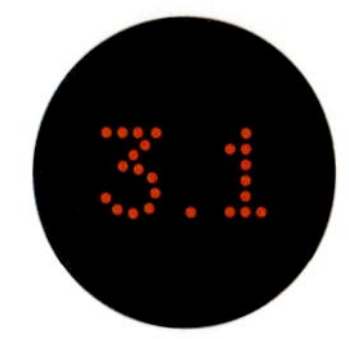

When reading the book of Ephesians, it's important to remember that this book was not written primarily to leaders, a seminary or a professional church staff. Rather, it was written to average Christians who had been swept up into the gospel and found themselves in the middle of a full-blown movement that was spreading across the whole Asia Minor province and beyond (Acts 19:8-10).

As Paul wrote to this movement, he wanted to make sure the people in those churches knew that everyone had a role to play in keeping the movement going. Paul says in Ephesians 4:7, "To each one of us grace has been given according to the measure of Christ's gift." Paul is clear that everyone has received a gifting from Christ. This means every person in Christ has been given a measure of grace to represent the ministry of Christ. This is revolutionary because it puts the power and authority to represent Christ back into the hands of ordinary people. Everyone gets to play—no one is a spectator.

If this weren't revolutionary enough, it goes even deeper and wider. If we can accept that in all of life (living systems), the potential for the whole is contained in the smallest part, then we can say that each one of us contains the potential of all five vocations/giftings. This idea may seem radical, but it begins to make sense with this example: In genetics, each cell only uses a part of the whole coding but contains all the embedded DNA and its capacity to replicate. In a very real sense, there is an orchard in every apple. What Paul seems to say in Ephesians 4 is that **we have the potential for all five ministries within us, but they have been given to each one of us in different measures.**

COACHING MOMENT

Acknowledging that the potential to function in all aspects of APEST is in us does not mean we will function in all five of these giftings with the same degree of effectiveness. Experience tells us that no one is fully competent in all five. Only Jesus functioned as a fully mature apostle, prophet, evangelist, shepherd and teacher. Our potential for operating effectively in each of the five will depend on the measure of grace we have received from Christ in each area, as well as the level of equipping we receive from the other ministries.

The key to understanding this principle is understanding that we have all five giftings in different measures. So for example, my (Tim) APEST profile looks something like this:

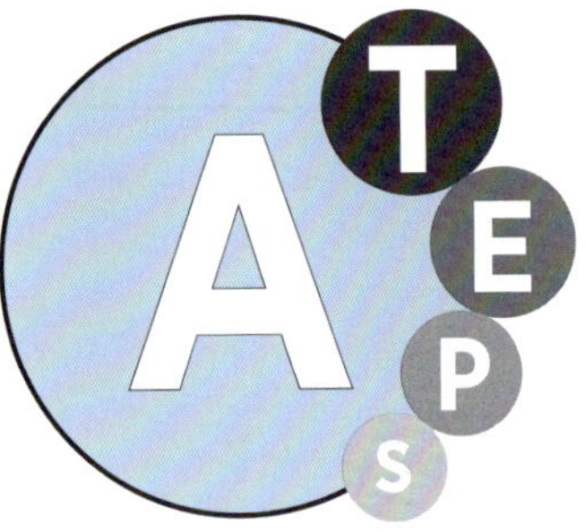

My primary (base) ministry is that of an apostle (one who is sent and extends). My secondary ministry gifting is that of a teacher, and so on down the list. Notice how each circle gets smaller as it goes down the right side of the larger circle? The measure of gifting I have received as a shepherd is significantly less than the measure of gifting I have received as an evangelist. I can function in a shepherding role, but I will not be as effective at shepherding as someone who has a primary (base) gifting of shepherd.

Notes

Scripture says that Christ measured, or apportioned, our gifting to us. Why do you think he chose to give us all a different measure of gifting?

Why not give every person the same measure?

Ephesians 3:17 says that Christ dwells in our hearts by faith. Is it difficult for you to believe that the capacity to function in all five APEST ministries dwells within you?

Why or why not?

If each person in your group has the capacity to function in all five ministries at varying levels of effectiveness, what does this say about the capacity of your group to represent the fullness of Christ?

3.2 MEDITATION // Personal APEST Profiles

Thinking about all five of the APEST giftings as being within us can be an exciting discovery! It means Christ has placed the full potential for revolutionary impact within each one of us. Just as a seed contains the full potential for a tree, and the tree contains the full potential for a forest, so each believer contains the potential for the whole. One person can start a new church because all the genetics of an ecclesia (the church)—the Holy Spirit and the gospel, social connections and ministry (including APEST)—is contained within him or her. That new church can start other churches, and before long a movement is born. This is how God has worked through his church in times past, and this is how he can work through us now. Each part contains the potential for the whole, and the whole is made up of each part. Christ has given us everything we need to be a permanent revolution.

This is an exciting discovery, recognizing that all five ministries are present within each one of us, and it also helps us make sense of the confusion we sometimes have about what our primary gifting is. One way to find clarity in this area is to ask yourself two questions: "What energizes me?" and, "What's the biggest problem in the church?"

What energizes me?

Paul says in Ephesians 4:16 that there is an "effectual working" within each one of us. The word he uses in that phrase is the Greek word *energia*, from which the English word *energy* derives. Paul is saying that each person has a certain energy that, when it is operating, contributes to the growth and maturity of the body.

When you operate within your primary calling (gifting), you operate out of a certain energy and grace that has been given to you by Christ. As we discussed in week 2, your ministry calling is literally built into the way you are designed. It is a lifelong calling and vocation. Discerning the kinds of ministry opportunities that energize you is often a good indicator as to how Christ has shaped you for ministry.

For example, a prophet will be energized by engaging in ministries that focus on prayer, hearing from God and serving the poor and disadvantaged. An apostle will be energized by starting new ventures that involve design, innovation and laying new foundations. A teacher will be stimulated by opportunities to learn and explain truth. Those who are animated by opportunities to share the gospel are likely to be evangelists. And those energized by ministries that foster intimacy and belonging are often gifted as shepherds.

What is the biggest problem in the church?

We see the world as filled with projects that we are capable of doing. As a result, we often point out gaps in the church that, without us realizing, point to how we are uniquely designed to fill those gaps. In other words, how we define the church's problems is typically a reflection of our own gifting.

For example, when you ask a teacher what the biggest problem in the church is, he might answer by saying that people don't know their Bibles well enough. If you ask an evangelist the same question, she will probably say the main problem is that we are not sharing the gospel and recruiting others to the cause.

Sometimes the problems we see in the church are a direct reflection of the way Christ has gifted us for ministry. Our gifting shapes how we see the problem and then provides a distinctive approach for solving that problem as well.

COACHING MOMENT

Discovering our primary calling is not to be done in isolation. Your group, as well as those who know you best, should play a part in helping you discern how you are shaped for ministry.

Notes

What energizes you and how you define the main problem in the church are often a good starting points for discerning what your primary gifting is. List below the kinds of ministry activities that energize you, along with what you think the biggest problem in the church is. Try to narrow down what you think this reveals about your primary calling for ministry. Feel free to reference the list of detailed APEST definitions in the front of the book and to ask others how they think you would answer these questions.

What kinds of ministry activities energize you?

What does this possibly reveal about what your primary calling (gifting) is?

What would you say the biggest problem in the church is?

What does this possibly reveal about what your primary calling (gifting) is?

Paul says in Ephesians 4:7 that each one of us has been given a measure of gifting from Christ. When you think about the measure of gifting that Christ has given you in each of the five APEST ministries, what would you say is your primary calling? What about your secondary calling? Fill out the graph below with what you think your primary APEST gifting is in the largest circle, your secondary gifting in the next largest circle, and so on.

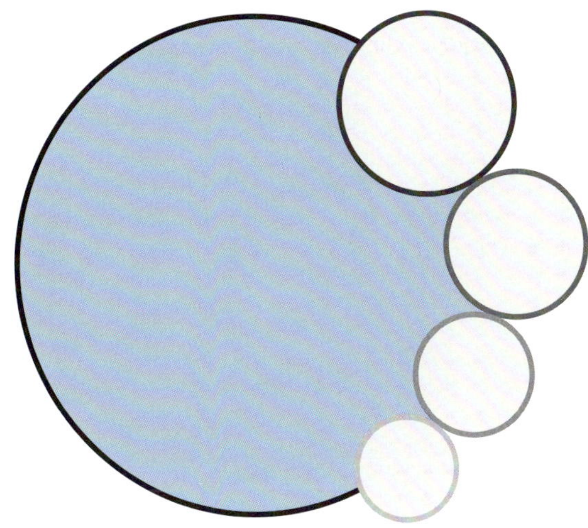

When you think about all five APEST giftings being in you, how does this make you feel? Explain.

If the capacity to function in all five APEST ministries is within each one of us, what are the implications for the roles each one of you play in the group?

Groups are typically formed in order to face a particular challenge or solve a particular problem. As you think about the group you are (or will be) in, what particular challenges has this group chosen to focus on?

What do you think this reveals about the possible APEST ministry callings represented in the group?

Sometimes, when we are introduced to something like APEST we begin to feel as though someone is trying to put us into a box. Saying that someone is an apostle or teacher or evangelist can sound like we are putting labels on people and overlooking how each person is uniquely shaped. No one likes to be put in a box, and we all know a one-size-fits-all approach rarely works with anything. So recognizing that all five APEST ministries, in various measures, are within in each one of us helps account for the complexity of how each person is uniquely designed. Just as a kaleidoscope combines the same fragments in various ways to form unique designs, the different APEST giftings all combine differently within each person to form a unique and complex ministry profile.

For example, a prophet with a secondary gifting of teaching will function differently from a teacher with a secondary gifting of prophet. The prophet-teacher will tend to use the Scriptures to focus people on God's values and reality, calling people to a higher standard. The teacher-prophet, on the other hand, will likely emphasize the power of the Scriptures themselves and the importance of doctrine as a means of being faithful to God. Both are interested in truth, but their approach to ministry, and even their approach to the Scriptures themselves, will be different.

Each measure of gifting, when combined with the others, will produce a particular gifting set within each person. We did the math, and APEST can be combined a total of 120 different ways. That's 120 possible vocational profiles! APEST may seem simple on the surface, but the deeper you delve into it, the more rich and complex it gets. There is plenty of diversity within the APEST typologies to account for the variety of our distinctive callings and personalities.

COACHING MOMENT

Even within these 120 different combinations within APEST, there are different measures of grace given to each person in their respective APEST ministry profile. So even if two people have the same ministry profile of PTSEA, they will not necessarily have the same measure of grace given to them in each category of gifting. While they both may be gifted primarily as prophets, their measure of gifting as prophets will be different. This will nuance and flavor each of their respective ministries, influencing their overall vibe and impact. When this is factored into the equation, it is easy to see why no two people are the same, regardless of their APEST ministry profile.

Notes

No one likes to feel as if they are being forced into a box. Why is it important to recognize the potential variety of gifting combinations within each person (120 in all)?

Thinking about all five of the APEST giftings being within us provokes a new way of seeing ourselves and those in our group. How does this change the way you see your own abilities to engage in different forms of ministry?

How does this change the way you see your group?

3.4

ACTION // Personal APEST Profiles

It's now time to take the "light" version of the *APEST Ministry Profile Test.* Go to the back of the *Playbook* and fill out the chart on page 152. Those looking for a more in-depth, comprehensive analysis of personal and group profiles can take an online *APEST Assessment* at *www.apest.org.* After you have taken one of the tests, fill in the diagram below based on your results.

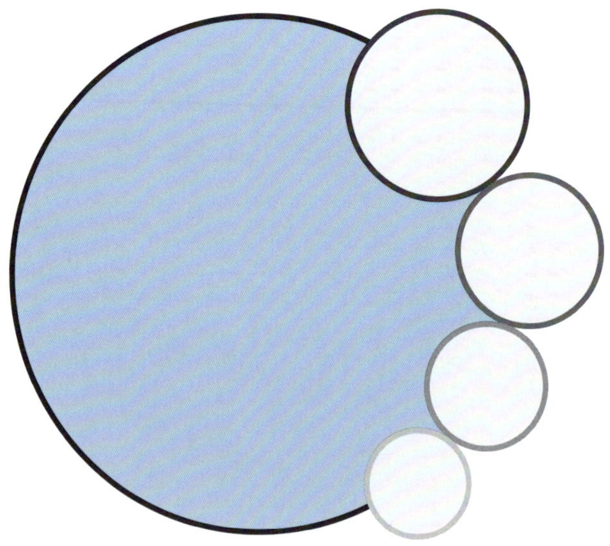

COACHING MOMENT

It is important that you take the test today and bring the results with you to share during your Synergy Day tomorrow. This way, everyone one will be able to observe the results of how the assessment depicts each group member's gifts.

3.5

SYNERGY // Personal APEST Profiles

Today the group gets to discuss their ministry profiles with one another. Each person should have taken the *APEST Ministry Profile Test* and filled in the diagram in day 3.4 to share with the group.

> For this reason I bow my knees before the Father, from whom every family in heaven and on earth is named, that according to the riches of his glory he may grant you to be strengthened with power through his Spirit in your inner being, so that Christ may dwell in your hearts through faith—that you, being rooted and grounded in love, may have strength to comprehend with all the saints what is the breadth and length and height and depth, and to know the love of Christ that surpasses knowledge, that you may be filled with all the fullness of God.
> **(Ephesians 3:14–19 ESV)**

However, before you share your results with the rest of the group, discuss the following questions:

On the first day (3.1), we talked about how all five APEST giftings are within each one of us. Share with the group how you answered this question: Ephesians 3:17 says that Christ dwells in our hearts by faith.

Is it difficult for you to believe that all five APEST ministries dwell in you?

Why or why not?

On day two (3.2), we thought about how each of the five APEST giftings may show up in us, from primary to secondary and all the way down the right side of the circle. Share with the group how you filled out the diagram on page 65 and explain why you filled it out in that order.

Sharing APEST Ministry Profile Reports

Take some time for each person to share the results of their *APEST Ministry Profile Test*. At minimum, everyone should share what their primary (base) ministry is, along with some insights from their report that they thought were helpful to them.

Feel free to ask each other questions and comment on what other group members share. This is a time to be transparent and build awareness within your team about how Christ has shaped each one of you for ministry. Here are some suggested questions you can ask each other to help increase awareness:

What parts of your profile do you see as being accurate? Why?

What parts of your profile do you feel misrepresent you at this time? Why?

Have you learned anything new about yourself in this process? If so, what did you learn?

Give constructive feedback to each other. You could say something like, "You say that you are a primary teacher but I experience you as a primary prophet and here's why."

APEST is simple (five ministry giftings) and yet complex (120 possible variations) all at the same time. Share with the group how you answered this question: No one likes to feel as if they are being forced into a box. Why is it important to recognize the potential variety of gifting combinations within each person (120 in all)?

Developing an APEST Group Profile

Now that you have shared the results from your personal profiles, it's time to develop a ministry profile for your group. Knowing your group's ministry profile can help explain a lot of things about the group. If your team shares a lot of the same primary giftings, it may explain why the group gravitates toward certain kinds of ministry opportunities. It may also explain why your group experiences challenges in certain areas.

Name:

List top two gifts in order:

Name:

List top two gifts in order:

Name:

List top two gifts in order:

Name:

List top two gifts in order:

Name:

List top two gifts in order:

Name:

List top two gifts in order:

Name:

List top two gifts in order:

Name:

List top two gifts in order:

Group Score: Add up the total times each gift is represented from the chart.

Apostolic

Prophetic

Evangelist

Shepherd

Teacher

COACHING MOMENT

If you do not have all five APEST giftings represented in your group at the primary level, it does not mean you cannot be effective as a group. Regardless of the variations of gifting represented within your group, you can still function with a spirit of unity and service. Remember, we all have all five giftings within us.

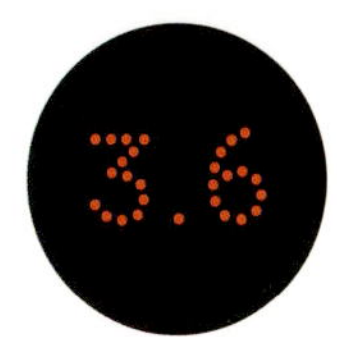

Understanding APEST gives us an insight into how the body of Christ works in communities of any size. Being able to recognize how Christ has gifted each one of us is an important step toward functioning as the body of Christ. If you don't know what your primary gifting is, you probably won't know how valuable you are to the life and maturity of the community. In the same way, if you don't recognize how Christ has gifted others in the body, then you will likely take them for granted or, even worse, reject them for being gifted differently than you are. Understanding APEST is, at the very least, understanding how valuable each person is and coming to a place where we can open ourselves up to each other and receive a measure of Christ in doing so.

This leads to a warning: When only one or two giftings dominate a community, the community inevitably gets cloned by those who have the most influence in the group. The most charismatic person becomes the point of reference for what legitimate spirituality, ministry and leadership look like.

When this happens, it has a way of making others with different giftings wonder if there is something wrong with them, or if there is even a place for them in the body. The body becomes fractured and, as a result, unable to mature. Obviously, this is not the way God designed his community to operate.

Each one of us is gifted by Christ to represent a measure of his ministry. Christ designed the body of Christ to have a diversity of giftings yet serve with unity in the Spirit (Ephesians 4:1-2). To use an example from physics, when we are able to recognize diversity of giftings

Now to him who is able to do immeasurably more than all we ask or imagine, according to his power that is at work within us, to him be glory in the church and in Christ Jesus throughout all generations, for ever and ever! Amen. **(Ephesians 3:20–21)**

(fission) and still function with a level of unity that allows each part to contribute to the whole (fusion), we will unleash an enormous amount of energy (nuclear) within the body of Christ. God will, in the words of Ephesians 3:20-21, be able to do more than all we ask or imagine.

Consider this passage from 1 Peter 4:10-11:

> *Each of you should use whatever gift you have received to serve others, as faithful stewards of God's grace in its various forms. If anyone speaks, they should do so as one who speaks the very words of God. If anyone serves, they should do so with the strength God provides, so that in all things God may be praised through Jesus Christ. To him be the glory and the power for ever and ever. Amen.*

Recognizing the diversity of gifting within the body can be exciting. Knowing that the ministry of Christ is fully represented in the body of Christ is quite a revolutionary discovery. And there is one more area in which recognizing the diversity of giftings in APEST can help us grow. We are all reactionary creatures by nature, and so there is a temptation, when looking at giftings, to think we 1) have to be good at all five, or 2) that we are not good at any of them.

The beautiful thing about Ephesians 4 is that it teaches us to accept our APEST ministry profile as a gift of grace. No one is going to be good at all five. If you are primarily gifted as a prophet, you may not be naturally good at evangelizing, even though at times you are called to evangelize. If you are primarily gifted as a shepherd, you may not be naturally good at teaching, even though you are called to be able to articulate what you believe in a theologically consistent way.

Recognizing that we are all given a certain measure of grace releases us from trying to be the total package. It's okay if you are not gifted as a teacher. It's okay if you are not gifted as an evangelist. It's okay if you are

We do not dare to classify or compare ourselves with some who commend themselves. When they measure themselves by themselves and compare themselves with themselves, they are not wise.
(2 Corinthians 10:12)

not primarily gifted as an apostle. Christ has gifted you with a measure of grace to be who he has designed you to be. In the words of Peter, you can minster out of the strength God provides. You don't have to compare yourself with people who have different measures of gifting than you do. You can accept yourself and those around you for who God made them to be.

You can only be who you were designed to be. No more, no less. Embracing the truth of Ephesians 4 allows us to escape our tendency to compare ourselves with one another, be competitive or even be condemning of ourselves or others for being different.

Spend a moment thanking Christ for the grace he has given you to serve.

// Pioneers and Settlers

Trying to figure out the primary way in which Christ has gifted you for ministry can be challenging. I (Tim) can remember having a tough time figuring out whether I was an evangelist or an apostle. I had always had my heart set on reaching people who were not Christians with the good news of Jesus, but I also found myself being drawn toward doing evangelism in cultures that were different from my own. To top it off, I did not just want to help someone find Jesus: I wanted to start little groups of new Jesus-followers all over the place.
So which was it? Was I an evangelist or an apostle?

This same kind of confusion can take place when someone is trying to figure out if he is a teacher or a prophet. Both the teacher and the prophet are concerned about communicating truth, but they have a different way of going about it and can be motivated by very different reasons.

For most of my life, if you had explained the APEST roles to me, I would have considered myself a teacher. In my career, I taught English in the classroom for nearly twenty years. In ministry, I often taught Bible classes or Sunday school classes, with some occasional preaching. But over time, I realized that my interest in communicating truth was not primarily from an educational standpoint. Rather, I was primarily looking to speak truth into a particular situation within the group. It needed to be a word in season, on target for that particular situation. In other words, it needed to be incarnational. This is one of the reasons why I now see my vocation in the body as more of a prophet than a teacher. (Jeff Darnell)

COACHING MOMENT

The prophet, like the teacher, is passionate about truth but in a different way. The prophet is looking to incarnate God's reality in the here and now. It needs to be fleshed out in tangible, concrete ways that address the gap between God's reality and ours. Truth for the prophet is truth applied for a particular place and time, while truth for a teacher tends to be more abstract and universal.

While discovering your primary ministry is not always easy, we've found that discussing one's posture toward the local expression of the church and society can often provide various clues. For example, do you like to spend a lot of time and energy at the center of the community? Or are you drawn toward ministry opportunities that take place away from the center toward the edge?

The center of the church community is not only where you find Christians gathered together, it's also where you typically find more structure and organization. Some people like to spend a lot of time with Christians. They feel drawn toward the kinds of ministries that provide for the needs of those in the church and help keep the church up and running. Others feel called to invest more time and energy in people and places that are found further from the center of the church and its gatherings. They are energized by moving toward the edge of the community where they can encounter new people, experiences and environments.

One way of describing people who are either drawn to the center or the edge is to use the language of settlers and pioneers. Those who feel called to invest more time and energy at the center can be called settlers. Settlers prefer a more predictable environment where routines and practices have literally been "settled" and now have a proven track record. Those who feel called to spend more time toward the edge can be called pioneers.
If we apply this notion of pioneers and settlers to

APEST, we find an interesting comparison. Here is how it could be drawn out in a diagram:

The circle in the diagram represents the local Christian community. The teachers and shepherds are the ones who are most at home at the center of the community. Their ministries tend to take place on a more local level. The evangelist typically has one foot in the community and one foot out. In their quest for new social encounters, the evangelist ventures outside the boundaries of the settlement and explores new relational frontiers. However, they typically do not go too far from the center. They are like bees that leave the hive, roam around, and eventually come back to home base. This pattern of coming in and going out gives their ministries a supra-local quality.

When it comes to distance from the center, the prophet tends to be a couple steps in front of the evangelist. The center is often culturally noisy, and for someone on a quest to hear from God, this poses quite a challenge. Their sensitivity to violations of the covenant can also lead the prophet to back away from the inconsistencies they perceive in the community. At the center we enter into closer proximity with one another. This opens up a window for us to see how people really are, which brings the community's moral and social deficits more clearly into focus. In an effort to resolve this tension between what is and what should be, prophets often withdraw from the group. Instead, they tend to be drawn to people on the margins, especially those who are overlooked by those at the center.

As the "sent one," the apostle is the one who is most energized by the thought of moving toward a frontier. Whether it's mobilizing the settlement to be more pioneering or launching out to start a new center on the edge, apostles are always strategizing about how to move into the next frontier. This tendency to cross boundaries is what often leads mature apostles to have a trans-local quality in their ministries.

COACHING MOMENT

The difference between an evangelist and an apostle can be summed up in what they are looking to accomplish. An evangelist is ultimately focused on bringing new people into relationship with Jesus and the Christian community. They do their best work when they can build on an existing foundation. Their ministry tends to be more interpersonal and aids in the individual conversion process. Apostles, on the other hand, are more like architects. They envision new endeavors from the ground up, which leads them to focus on the more foundational issues of organizational design and architecture (Romans 15:20-21; I Corinthians 3:10). As such, they have a higher capacity for systems thinking and the more structural concerns related to founding new ventures.

Notes

More details about the differences between settlers and pioneers may be helpful. In the table below, circle the phrases which best describe you.

Settlers tend to be more focused on...	**Pioneers tend to be more focused on...**
people in the church	people outside the church
maintaining what's already in place	starting new things
staying within the existing boundaries	crossing boundaries to explore
the present situation	future possibilities
keeping everyone together	keeping everyone moving
securing what we already have	pursuing what we don't have
putting down roots	breaking new ground

Using the language of pioneers and settlers is not a way to place people in two different camps and pit them against each other. There are natural tensions that exist in the body of Christ between people who have different postures toward the center and the edge. Using the language of pioneers and settlers helps us understand this tension and provides a healthy framework to talk about it. Sometimes simply having terminology to describe what is going on can help us negotiate the challenges at hand.

Based on this table, would you say you are more of a settler or a pioneer? Why?

How about your team? Is it predominantly made up of pioneers, settlers or a mix of both?

4.2 MEDITATION // Pioneers and Settlers

The story of America is a story about pioneers and settlers. Lewis and Clark were the first pioneering leaders to go all the way from the east coast to the west coast and back again. They opened the journey into what we now call the Old West. So who is responsible for the expansion into the Old West? Was it the pioneers or the settlers? The answer is both! The pioneers moved into the unknown and discovered new territories. The settlers followed close behind and established new settlements. It was a great partnership that proved to be highly influential in American history.

One thing we learn from this portion of American history is that pioneers and settlers need each other. Without the pioneers, we would never break out of our existing settlements and move into new frontiers. Without the settlers, the new territory discovered by the pioneers would remain undeveloped and drift back toward being a frontier. Pioneers and settlers need to work together if we are going to experience a sustainable breakthrough.

COACHING MOMENT

The challenge in keeping settlers and pioneers working together is that they are prone to focus on things that pull them in different directions. Pioneers embrace the "new" and move toward the frontier, which creates opportunities for people at the center to encounter the edge. When the center opens itself up to engaging the edge, they enter into a growth process that helps the center become more adaptable to the challenges of the frontier. Just as our own bodies grow stronger from being stretched and exposed to new environments, the body of Christ grows and matures when it reaches beyond the settlement and engages new and unfamiliar experiences on the frontier. Without the pioneering ministries of the APEs, the settlement will lose its adaptive edge and ultimately turn inward and become fixated on its own needs, turning a blind eye to the hurting world around it.

Notes

Any time we introduce diversity into a group, it's important to emphasize the things we have in common. In Ephesians 4:4-6 Paul says:

> *There is one body and one Spirit, just as you were called to one hope when you were called; one Lord, one faith, one baptism; one God and Father of all, who is over all and through all and in all.*

Here, Paul gives us a list of seven "ones" that form the basis of our unity in Christ. List those seven ones below:

1.

2.

3.

4.

5.

6.

7.

Finally, all of you, be like-minded, be sympathetic, love one another, be compassionate and humble. **(1 Peter 3:8)**

Recognizing the unity we have in Christ positions us to embrace the diversity within our team. Spend a few moments meditating on the things you have in common with those on your team.

If you are a settler, think about a time when you worked with a pioneer(s). What was challenging about that experience?

What did you learn from it?

If you are a pioneer, think about a time when you worked with a settler(s). What was challenging about that experience?

What did you learn from it?

COACHING MOMENT

Be honest with the questions above, because this exercise helps the entire team understand each other. You will be asked to share some of your answers on Synergy Day.

The "Growing" Tension between Pioneers and Settlers

Paul knew we would struggle to embrace the diversity of giftings in the body. The tensions between settlers and pioneers can be pretty intense. Each group thinks that their ministry focus is the most important one, often to the exclusion of the others. Part of the way the APEST giftings help us mature is by forcing us to live with this tension. Pioneers need the settlers, and the settlers need the pioneers.

It seems that this tension was at the front of Paul's mind when he started writing Ephesians 4. He commands us:

> *...walk worthy of the calling with which you were called, with all lowliness and gentleness, with longsuffering, bearing with one another in love, endeavoring to keep the unity of the Spirit in the bond of peace.* (Ephesians 4:1-3 NKJV)

Notice he says that we have to endeavor to keep the unity of the Spirit. Embracing diversity in the group can be really difficult. It requires us to open ourselves up to new language, new perspectives and new values. This will require us to bear with one another in love and make a real effort to understand each other.

Therefore, as God's chosen people, holy and dearly loved, clothe yourselves with compassion, kindness, humility, gentleness and patience. Bear with each other and forgive one another if any of you has a grievance against someone. Forgive as the Lord forgave you. And over all these virtues put on love, which binds them all together in perfect unity. Let the peace of Christ rule in your hearts, since as members of one body you were called to peace. And be thankful.
(Colossians 3:12–15)

Notes

Why do you pass judgment on your brother? Or you, why do you despise your brother? For we will all stand before the judgment seat of God; for it is written, "As I live, says the Lord, every knee shall bow to me, and every tongue shall confess to God." So then each of us will give an account of himself to God. **(Romans 14:10–12 ESV)**

Pioneers often tend to overlook and even look down on the role that settlers play in helping the church grow and mature. If you are a pioneer, list 5 reasons why settlers are important to the body of Christ in the space below. If you are settler, go to the next question.

1.

2.

3.

4.

5.

Coaching Moment For Pioneers

From a visionary standpoint, pioneers often see both the settlement and the frontier, while settlers tend to focus more on the local needs of the settlement. As a pioneer you need to understand that not everyone moves as quickly and easily in the face of opportunity as you do. Settlers may not have a problem with moving into the frontier, but they need to know more details. Settlers need to have a clear picture of where the pioneer wants to go and how they plan on getting there. Often settlers will come along for the journey if they know what specific steps they need to take. This means it is the responsibility of the pioneer, when possible, to set a practical step-by-step process describing what the pioneering journey will look like. This is one of the ways settlers help pioneers mature: They lead pioneers to develop the patience and discipline to move in a way that lets everyone make the journey together.

Now we ask you, brothers and sisters, to acknowledge those who work hard among you, who care for you in the Lord and who admonish you. Hold them in the highest regard in love because of their work. Live in peace with each other. **(1 Thessalonians 5:12–13)**

Settlers can be tempted to underestimate and even resist the role that pioneers play in helping the community grow and mature. If you're a settler, list 5 reasons why we need pioneers in the body of Christ in the space below.

1.

2.

3.

4.

5.

Coaching Moment For Settlers

Hearing a pioneer talk about moving toward the frontier can be disturbing to settlers for several reasons. First, it can appear as if the pioneer is saying nothing good is happening at the settlement. Even though this is often not the case, settlers may take offense that the pioneers are not recognizing the hard work happening right underneath their noses. Second, settlers specialize in bringing stability to the community through consistency and order. Making a journey toward the frontier means the established routines at the settlement will be disrupted by new and unpredictable influences, making things feel a bit chaotic.

So then, welcome him in the Lord with great joy, and honor people like him, because he almost died for the work of Christ. He risked his life to make up for the help you yourselves could not give me. **(Philippians 2:29-30)**

Settlers have to remember that God has called his people to be on mission and to journey out into the unknown with him. At the edge, where order fades into chaos, we are forced to rely on God's grace and provision. Moving into the frontier means taking risks and exposing yourself to new challenges. This is one of the ways pioneers help settlers mature: Settlers have to open themselves up to the unsettling experience of moving toward the frontier. This requires sacrifice and courage.

Do everything without grumbling or arguing, so that you may become blameless and pure, "children of God without fault in a warped and crooked generation." Then you will shine among them like stars in the sky... **(Philippians 2:14–15)**

Briefly describe what your church would be like if no one was doing any shepherding or teaching. What kinds of challenges would your church face?

In the same vein, briefly describe what you think your church would be like if no one was doing any evangelistic, prophetic or apostolic ministry. What kinds of challenges would your church experience?

Every team will experience some form of tension or conflict. This is completely normal and can even be healthy. How does recognizing the realities of pioneers and settlers help you understand existing (or past) conflicts within your team?

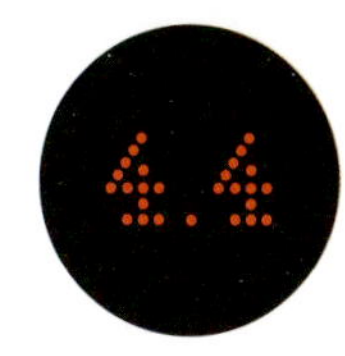

By now you realize that some of the conflicts we have in the body of Christ come as a result of the tension between settlers and pioneers. The settlers hunker down at the settlement and look at the pioneers with suspicion. The pioneers look at the settlers with frustration and often leave the settlement without them, launching out into the frontier on their own. This fractures the body of Christ and stunts our ability to grow and mature.

It's no accident that, in the middle of his discussion of APEST, Paul reminded the Ephesians (and us!) to speak the truth in love (Eph. 4:16). Each one of the giftings has a different way of seeing things. This in itself can be the beginning of conflict in a group. We must work through this tension between pioneers and settlers and realize through the process how valuable each person is to the body of Christ. This will require both pioneers and settlers to change how they see each other. If we truly see each other as essential parts of the body, it will affect how we talk to and about one another.

Most likely, you have a mix of pioneers and settlers on your team. Remember that *each one of us* has been gifted by Christ. Pioneers and settlers have to learn how to understand each other and work together. That leads to a simple action today.

If you are a pioneer, approach someone on your team who you think might be a settler and let him or her know why he or she is valuable to the team.

Let us therefore make every effort to do what leads to peace and to mutual edification. **(Romans 14:19)**

Therefore encourage one another and build each other up, just as in fact you are doing.
(1 Thessalonians 5:11)

If you are a settler, approach someone on your team who you think might be a pioneer and let him or her know why he or she is valuable to the team.

Do this before your Synergy Day tomorrow.

After your group has had time to hang out and socialize, start with some of these discussion questions.

We opened the week by noting the difference between pioneers and settlers. Which one of these metaphors best describes your team? Explain why.

On day two (4.2), we talked about how pioneers and settlers tend to move in different directions. Have you ever experienced this tension? If so, what was it like?

On day three (4.3), we looked at some things that needed to change in order for us to grow and mature from this tension. If you are a pioneer, we asked you to list reasons why settlers are valuable, and vice versa. Share those answers with the group and discuss them.

On day four (4.4), we highlighted the need for tension between pioneers and settlers. This tension will only be healthy if we learn to speak the truth in love. Which area do you think your team needs to grow in the most? Speaking truth to one another, or speaking truth in loving ways? Explain.

End your meeting with a prayer asking God to help you experience greater levels of unity and love for one another.

If I speak in the tongues of men or of angels, but do not have love, I am only a resounding gong or a clanging cymbal. If I have the gift of prophecy and can fathom all mysteries and all knowledge, and if I have a faith that can move mountains, but do not have love, I am nothing. If I give all I possess to the poor and give over my body to hardship that I may boast, but do not have love, I gain nothing. Love is patient, love is kind. It does not envy, it does not boast, it is not proud. It does not dishonor others, it is not self-seeking, it is not easily angered, it keeps no record of wrongs. Love does not delight in evil but rejoices with the truth. It always protects, always trusts, always hopes, always perseveres.
(1 Corinthians 13:1–7)

4.6 CALIBRATE // Pioneers and Settlers

> Do nothing out of selfish ambition or vain conceit. Rather, in humility value others above yourselves, not looking to your own interests but each of you to the interests of the others. **(Philippians 2:3-4)**

> We who are strong ought to bear with the failings of the weak and not to please ourselves. Each of us should please our neighbors for their good, to build them up. **(Romans 15:1-2)**

If the founding of America is a story of pioneers and settlers, then the story of the church in the west has largely been a story of the settlers wondering what to do with the pioneers. Because of how they are designed for ministry, we've seen that pioneers and settlers often see life, ministry and the church from totally different perspectives. To the settlers, the pioneers are a bit strange and even appear to be reckless at times. To the pioneers, the settlers seem shortsighted and overly fixated on past and present realities. Those at the settlement have often used this excuse to ignore the pioneers. The pioneers, in turn, reject the settlers, leaving the body of Christ fractured, divided and unable to grow and mature into the fullness of Christ.

Christ has gifted the church with both pioneers and settlers for a reason. The ministries of settlers (STs) help hold people together and make sure the operations of the church run smoothly and efficiently. The ministries of pioneers (APEs) help the church pursue its mission and effectively meet the challenges of the day. Both pioneers and settlers play an important role in helping the church be the permanent revolution that Jesus has called us to be.

Only when pioneers and settlers endeavor to keep the unity of the Spirit in the bond of peace can the church hope to see the kind of revolutionary impact that characterized the ministry of Jesus and the early Christian movement.

Notes

Take a moment to read Jesus' prayer in John 17:20-23:

> *My prayer is not for them alone. I pray also for those who will believe in me through their message, that all of them may be one, Father, just as you are in me and I am in you. May they also be in us so that the world may believe that you have sent me. I have given them the glory that you gave me, that they may be one as we are one— I in them and you in me—so that they may be brought to complete unity. Then the world will know that you sent me and have loved them even as you have loved me.*

After you read the prayer, try praying this same prayer for your team. Ask the Father to help your team experience unity and love for one another.

4.7 RE-CREATE // Pioneers and Settlers

Consider this Ephesians 4:16 passage again: “From him the whole body, joined and held together by every supporting ligament, grows and builds itself up in love, as each part does its work” (Ephesians 4:16).

I (Tim) can remember when I was first introduced to the five-fold ministries of APEST. It definitely stretched my thinking. I could no longer see ministry or leadership in the church the same again. On one side of the coin, this was disturbing. “If there are five basic ministries in the church,” I said to myself, “and we are primarily accessing only two of them (ST), then how can we start re-activating the other three?” This was a challenging question for me to entertain, one that I have devoted a lot of time and energy to answering.

On the other side of the coin, learning about how all five ministries can work together to help the body of Christ mature was a real source of energy and hope. Deep down, most of us know something is missing in our experience of ministry and leadership in the body of Christ. We know that we are meant to be and do so much more. Realizing the five-fold nature of the church’s ministry allows us to understand each other better and also shows us a way forward. The body of Christ can mature and become the permanent revolution we were meant to be. Christ has given us everything we need to get the job done.

Spend a moment thanking Christ for both the pioneers and the settlers in your church or ministry.

// Pathway to Maturity: Base and Phase

EXPLORATION // Pathway to Maturity: Base and Phase

The first part of this *Playbook* (weeks 1-4) was designed to help you broaden your understanding of ministry within the context of the body of Christ. Becoming familiar with how each one of us is designed for ministry creates a wonderful sense of self-awareness that powers us toward our personal callings. However, recognizing where we fit on the APEST spectrum is only the beginning.

The rest of this *Playbook* (weeks 5-6) will focus on how the diversity within APEST contributes to the overall effectiveness of the body of Christ. It's not enough to diversify our understandings of ministry—we also need to learn how to function as a body (and a team), with each part contributing to the whole. Luckily, we do not have to figure this out on our own. Ephesians 4:11-16 spells out with stark clarity exactly how the body of Christ attains maturity and becomes the fullness of Jesus in the world. Read this text from beginning to end—slowly.

> *So Christ himself gave the apostle, the prophets, the evangelists, the pastors and teachers, to equip his people for works of service, so that the body of Christ may be built up until we all reach unity in the faith and in the knowledge of the Son of God and become mature, attaining to the whole measure of the fullness of Christ. Then we will no longer be infants, tossed back and forth by the waves, and blown here and there by every wind of teaching and by the cunning and craftiness of people in their deceitful scheming. Instead, speaking the truth in love, we will grow to become in every respect the mature body of him who is the head, that is, Christ. From him the whole body, joined and held together by every supporting ligament, grows and builds itself up in love, as each part does its work.*

...being strengthened with all power according to his glorious might so that you may have great endurance and patience, and giving joyful thanks to the Father, who has qualified you to share in the inheritance of his holy people in the kingdom of light. **(Colossians 1:11-12)**

Paul says the overarching purpose of APEST is maturity, and that maturity happens through the process of equipping. The word Paul uses in verse 12 for "equip" is an interesting word. In some cases, it was used to describe the mending of torn fishing nets. In other cases, it was used to describe the process of setting a broken bone. Overall, the word carries the idea of increasing one's ability to function in a certain area. Paul is telling us that God gives each person APEST gifts so each person in the body of Christ can increase his or her ability to function within the five categories of Christ's ministry.

So for example, if you are a teacher, you are not just designed for teaching. (Remember, as we saw in week 3, you have all five APEST giftings to various degrees.) The other giftings in the body have been given to help prepare you to do what they do. So for a teacher, growing toward maturity means entering into a process of equipping by receiving training on how to function in the other four primary categories of ministry (APES).

To illustrate what this looks like, we use the language of Base and Phase. We all have a Base ministry in which we feel most comfortable. This Base ministry flows out of our primary gifting. In order to mature, we have to enter a Phase where we receive training and experience in one of the other four ministries. It would look something like this:

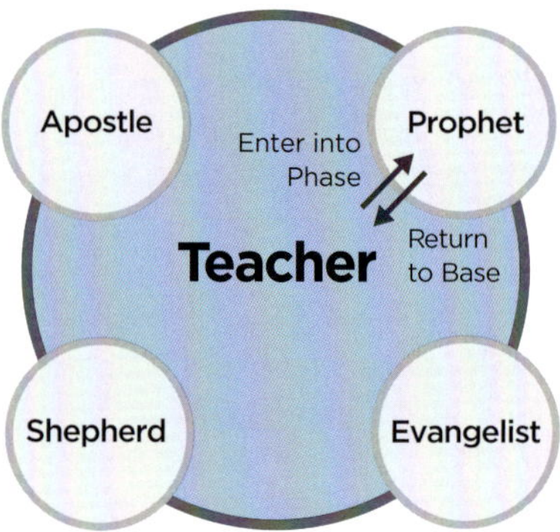

Ephesians 4 describes equipping as receiving training in how to function in one of the five APEST ministries. For this to happen, we must be exposed to people and ministry environments outside of our Base (primary) ministry. By participating in and receiving training for ministries at which we are not naturally gifted, we open ourselves up to a process of growth and maturity. So in the illustration on the previous page, a teacher enters into a prophetic Phase of ministry and receives training from another prophet(s) on how to function prophetically. After a Phase of being equipped by a prophet(s), the teacher returns to her Base ministry. Only now, instead of functioning solely as a teacher, she operates in her Base ministry of teaching with a fuller, more developed capacity to function prophetically as a teacher. This prophetic Phase will season and develop a teacher's ministry in ways that otherwise were not possible.

COACHING MOMENT

APEST gifts are not intended to function as ends in and of themselves. Being aware of how we are gifted for ministry is a big win, but it is only the starting point of a longer journey. In order for the church to mature and grow into the fullness of Christ, people with each of the APEST giftings have to equip others in the body to do what they do best. While someone gifted as a prophet may function prophetically within the body, this does not necessarily help the body to grow and mature into the fullness of Christ. The goal of APEST is not self-expression, but rather equipping others in the body to grow in their capacities to represent the full spectrum of Christ's ministry. Until a prophet begins to equip others to function prophetically, he has not fully lived into his calling as a prophet.

But you, keep your head in all situations, endure hardship, do the work of an evangelist, discharge all the duties of your ministry. **(2 Timothy 4:5)**

Base and Phase ministries work in this way:

- Not everyone is an apostle, but all of us are called to **live on mission.**

- Not everyone is a prophet, but everyone needs to know how to **listen to God.**

- Not everyone is an evangelist, but we're all called to **share the good news.**

- Not everyone is a shepherd, but **everyone is supposed to care.**

- Not everyone is a teacher, but we're all called to **share what we know.**

Our goal should be learning how to function in all five of the APEST ministries. No one will be good at all five. But we are called to grow in our capacity to function in the other ministries over our lifetimes. This is essentially what Paul means when he says that APEST helps the church mature into the fullness of Christ.

Ministry Vignette: Ben

When I was trying to discern my primary APEST vocation, I was initially drawn toward thinking I was an apostle. I have a history of starting new things and had recently planted a church. However, when I reflected on why I had planted a church, I began to realize that my primary motivation for planting a church was to somehow reform our notions of what the church is meant to be and do. I saw a gap between the "what should be" of God's kingdom and the "what is" of my city's current reality. This is a deeply prophetic impulse, noticing the gap between God's values and the current reality. What I came to realize was that my primary vocation was that of a prophet. I always had enough grace to function prophetically, but I would occasionally launch into an apostolic Phase in which I would have enough grace to do apostolic things for a season.

COACHING MOMENT

One of the keys to how APEST fosters maturity in the body is wrapped up in the word "exchange." Read the following verse of Ephesians 4:16 aloud:

> From him the whole body, joined and held together by every supporting ligament, grows and builds itself up in love, as each part does its work.

Paul gives us a vision of each person as both a giver and a receiver. We give training out of our strengths; we receive training in our weaknesses. The skills associated with each APEST ministry are distributed throughout the whole body, increasing the body's capacity to represent the full spectrum of Christ ministry in and through the church.

MEDITATION // Pathway to Maturity: Base and Phase

One of the challenging things about Ephesians 4 is that it forces us to wrestle with the possibility that we might not be as mature as we thought we were. If we have typically recognized only two or three of the five APEST giftings, then we are suddenly confronted with several other areas where we could experience growth. This is definitely a dose of humility for all involved!

Confronting us with areas where we need to grow and mature is exactly what the writer of Hebrews was doing when he said that the entire community should be teachers by now. Listen to what he says:

> *We have much to say about this, but it is hard to make it clear to you because you no longer try to understand. In fact, though by this time you ought to be teachers, you need someone to teach you the elementary truths of God's word all over again. You need milk, not solid food! Anyone who lives on milk, being still an infant, is not acquainted with the teaching about righteousness. But solid food is for the mature, who by constant use have trained themselves to distinguish good from evil.* (Hebrews 5:11-14)

Essentially, the writer is saying that his audience had been exposed to a competent teacher who had imparted to them the knowledge and skills that flow from that kind of ministry. But instead of them growing and maturing in the skills and understanding of that teacher, they had to continuously be taught the same things over and over again. They were continually dependent on the ministry of a teacher to give them what they need. According to the writer of Hebrews, this is a mark of immaturity.

Notes

The writer of Hebrews uses the metaphor of infants to illustrate his audience's lack of maturity in both their knowledge and skill to be teachers. It's like he was saying they were still hanging out in preschool when they should be graduating from high school. When you think about your current abilities to operate in the different APEST ministries, where would you locate yourself on the journey in each category of ministry? Are you still in preschool in some areas while demonstrating competence and maturity in others? On the continuums below, mark where you think you are in the maturing process for each ministry.

APOSTLE

Infancy - *Maturity*

PROPHET

Infancy - *Maturity*

EVANGELIST

Infancy - *Maturity*

SHEPHERD

Infancy - *Maturity*

TEACHER

Infancy - *Maturity*

No one will ever be fully mature in their Base ministry (primary gifting), much less in any of the other ministries. It takes time to enter into a Phase of ministry, learn from others, practice and experiment with it. Maturing into the fullness of Christ is a lifelong process.

COACHING MOMENT

What makes the maturing process even more challenging is many of us have not had access to the full spectrum of APEST ministries and leaders in order to learn and be equipped by them. The great thing about using the language of APEST is that it allows people to identify leaders or ministries from whom equipping can be received.

Take a moment to think about previous times in your life in which you may have entered into a Phase where you felt as though you were being equipped to do to a different kind of ministry.

Which APEST ministry was it?

How did you grow from that experience?

Take a moment to fill out the diagram on the following page. Put your Base (primary) ministry in the middle of the largest circle. Based on your previous experience, write down which particular APEST ministries you have entered into for Phases of equipping within the smaller circles. Then, in a few words, describe your growth experience in the box beside each Phase.

It takes a lifetime to mature. Most often we are not the ones who orchestrate a Phase in our life; instead, circumstances or a relationship typically guide us into it. The goal is not to agonize about your deficits or lack of experience in the various APEST ministries, but to remain open to entering a Phase and to embrace it when it happens. If the opportunity does not present itself, we can always seek out opportunities to learn from others.

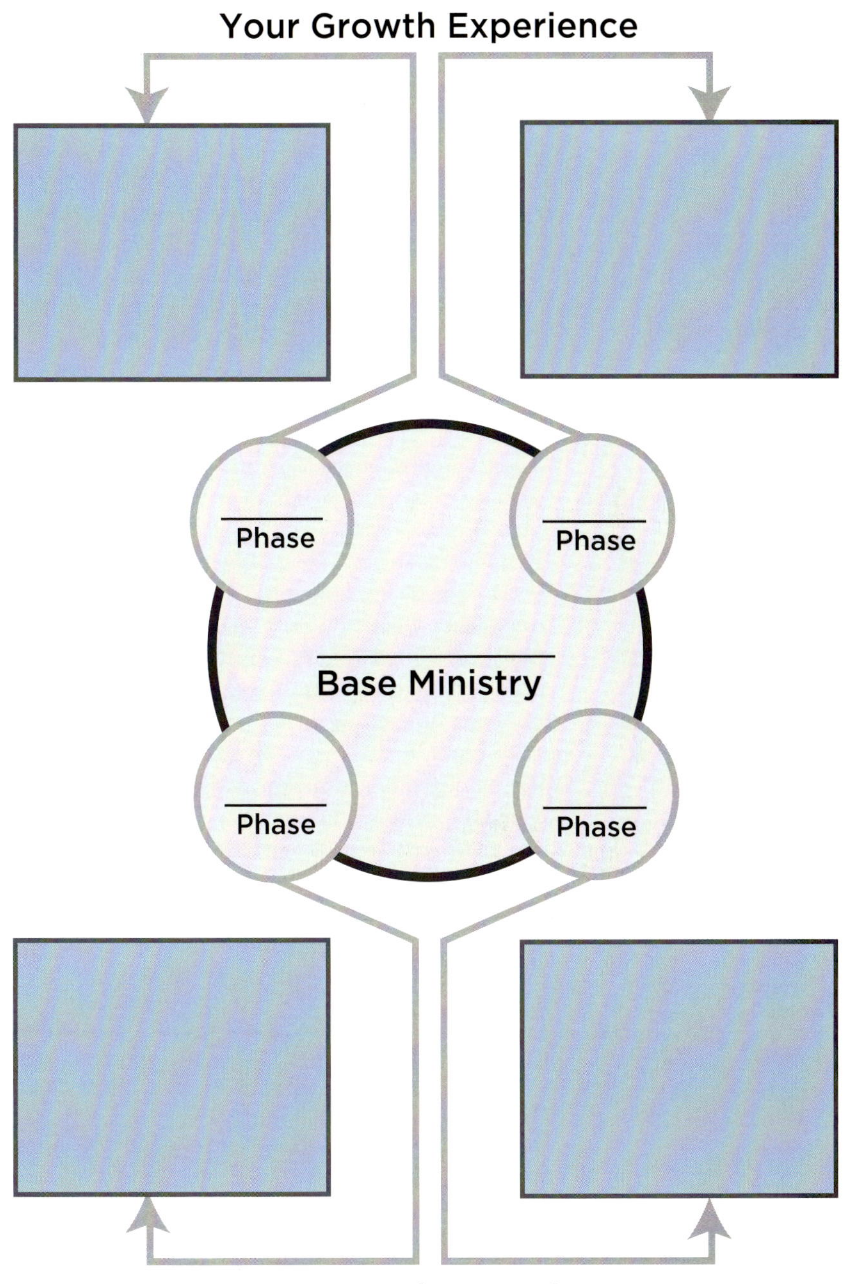
Your Growth Experience
Phase
Phase
Base Ministry
Phase
Phase
Your Growth Experience

CHANGE // Pathway to Maturity: Base and Phase

Ephesians 4 describes maturity in terms of developing competence in our ability to function in all five ministries of APEST. The journey toward maturity begins with exposure to the other giftings and the ministries that flow from them. Conventional wisdom tells us that we are supposed to find our strengths and only do things we are naturally good at. This sounds good at first, but it is not the way we mature. Just as our muscles grow when stretched and strained in proper ways, we experience growth when we allow ourselves to be stretched and strained by engaging in new ministry exercises, experiences and environments. The body of Christ does not exist solely for us to experience community; it's also the place where we are trained and equipped to become more competent in the skills and practices of mission and ministry.

The pathway to maturity is not easy, but we make that journey within community, where we can be encouraged by one another. As we open ourselves up to new experiences, we will find ourselves growing and maturing into the fullness of Christ both individually and as a community.

Notes

Paul tells Timothy, one of his team members left behind in the new church at Ephesus, to "do the work of an evangelist and fulfill your ministry" (2 Timothy 4:5). It's interesting to note that elsewhere Timothy was indirectly called an apostle: "Paul, Silas, and Timothy, To the church of the Thessalonians...we were not looking for praise from people, not from you or anyone else, even though as apostles of Christ we could have asserted our authority. Instead we were like young children among you" (1 Thessalonians 1:1;2:6-7). It seems that Paul's direction to Timothy at Ephesus was to function outside of his Base ministry of apostle and enter into a Phase of doing evangelistic ministry.

And say to Archippus, "See that you complete the ministry you have received in the Lord." **(Colossians 4:17)**

How have you typically approached doing things you are not good at? Choose from the options below, or write down your own response.

- ☐ *Refuse to do it*
- ☐ *Make excuses and find a way out*
- ☐ *Do it, but not try very hard*
- ☐ *Do it, but complain*
- ☐ *Jump in and try to grow from the new experience*
- ☐ ____________________

When we enter into a Phase, we must assume the posture of a learner. We will likely feel weak and incompetent, and may even appear that way to those around us. Based on how you answered the previous question, what do you need to do in order to open yourself up to experimenting with new forms of ministry?

Being in a Phase exposes our weakness and can often make us feel vulnerable and insecure. When someone in the group is in a Phase, it is a great opportunity for the other group members to support and encourage them through their season of growth. Read the following verse and answer the question below.

> *Do not let any unwholesome talk come out of your mouths, but only what is helpful for building others up according to their needs, that it may benefit those who listen.* (Ephesians 4:29)

Does your group naturally encourage one another, or is it more naturally sarcastic and cynical?

Why is it important for a group to develop an atmosphere of encouragement and support among its members?

How can your group develop this kind of atmosphere? What will need to happen?

Sometimes we enter a Phase of ministry because circumstances demand it. Maybe someone asks you to tell her more about Jesus and you suddenly enter into a Phase of evangelistic ministry. Maybe one of your friends calls you up and starts sharing some of his hurts and wounds with you. You are ushered into a Phase of shepherding where you need to show compassion and understanding and possibly walk with him through the healing process.

Entering a Phase of ministry does not always have to be spontaneous and unexpected. We can choose to open ourselves up to new experiences and intentionally enter into a Phase to seek out training to become more competent in a ministry. As I (Tim) write this, I have recently entered into a prophetic Phase of ministry with a guy I know who functions prophetically. After some prayer and reflection, I felt that I was supposed to approach him and ask if he would be open to me hanging out with him so I could learn more about how to do prophetic ministry. He was open to it, so we started hanging out once a week. While my Base ministry is not prophetic, I am learning how to function prophetically from someone who is naturally competent in that kind of ministry.

When we enter into a Phase of ministry, our competence to function in the other areas of ministry grows and moves us toward maturity. Base and Phase are ways of describing what it looks like for us to receive equipping from the other ministries to do what they do.

I hope in the Lord Jesus to send Timothy to you soon, so that I too may be cheered by news of you. For I have no one like him, who will be genuinely concerned for your welfare. For they all seek their own interests, not those of Jesus Christ. But you know Timothy's proven worth, how as a son with a father he has served with me in the gospel. **(Philippians 2:19–22 ESV)**

Being on a team gives you access to people who are more competent than you in different areas of ministry. Think about the people on your team.

Who is further along than you in one of the APEST ministries that you would like to learn from? Write that person's name below.

On Synergy Day, you will be asked to share that name and what ministry skills you would like to learn from them.

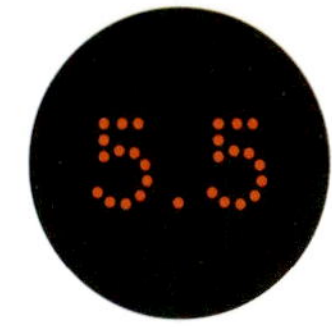

Let's review some of the content from the last few days. Answer the following questions together.

On the first day (5.1), we talked about how the APEST giftings are supposed to equip the rest of the body to "do what they do" so we can grow up in "every respect" (all things) in Christ. Have you ever heard someone, when presented with an opportunity to serve in a particular area, respond by saying "That's not my gifting, so I'm not going to do that"? or "I don't feel called to that, so I'll let someone else do it"? In light of Ephesians 4, when is this an appropriate response? When is this an inappropriate response? Explain.

On day two (5.2), you filled out a diagram on page 113 describing a time when you may have entered a Phase of equipping in another ministry. Share one of those Phases and the growth experience you had with the group.

On day three (5.3), we mentioned the importance of developing an atmosphere of support and encouragement in your group. Share with the group how you answered these two questions.

Does your group naturally encourage one another, or is it more naturally sarcastic and cynical?

Why is it important as a group to develop an atmosphere of encouragement and support?

Do not let any unwholesome talk come out of your mouths, but only what is helpful for building others up according to their needs, that it may benefit those who listen.
(Ephesians 4:29)

On day four (5.4), you were asked to think of someone in your group who is further along than you in a particular APEST ministry. Share with the group whose name you wrote down and what ministry skills you would like to learn from him or her. End your group time by asking the Father to help your team to become equippers of one another as the mature body of Christ should be.

The pathway to maturity mapped out in Ephesians 4, just like our own journeys toward maturity, is marked by new experiences and challenges. Learning how to do things we are not naturally good at can be a real challenge. It forces us to be humble and face our limitations. But this is part of what it means to be a disciple and live in community.

As disciples we are, by definition, learners. The very word implies that we don't have it all together. In community, we draw from one another and achieve amazing things that no one person could achieve on his or her own. Each one of us brings something to the table that helps the rest of the community grow and mature. In this way, each one of us is designed both to be equipped and to be equippers. We are both givers and receivers. I cannot grow and mature without you, and you cannot grow and mature without me.

Not that I have already obtained this or am already perfect, but I press on to make it my own, because Christ Jesus has made me his own. Brothers, I do not consider that I have made it my own. But one thing I do: forgetting what lies behind and straining forward to what lies ahead, I press on toward the goal for the prize of the upward call of God in Christ Jesus. Let those of us who are mature think this way, and if in anything you think otherwise, God will reveal that also to you.
(Philippians 3:12–15 ESV)

The terms Base and Phase help us understand how the process of equipping toward maturity takes place in the body of Christ. Sometimes God orchestrates our entry into a Phase, and sometimes we enter a Phase out of our own eagerness to grow and develop our competence for ministry. One thing is for sure: No one matures in all five simultaneously. It is a process that happens over a lifetime. While we will never be fully mature in all five, we can mature in our level of competence to function in all five. Both as individuals and collectively as the body of Christ, we can mature into the fullness of Christ and become the permanent revolution God designed us to be.

Notes

If we only do things we are naturally good at, we will never grow and mature into the fullness of Christ. In order to make the journey toward maturity, you have to demonstrate two things: humility and courage. Humility admits that there is room for you to grow and mature in your ability to function in the other ministries. Courage enters into new experiences and experiments with areas of ministry you are not naturally good at.

Which one of these two things do you struggle with the most?

Why?

Let's start by today by revisiting a passage of Scripture from Ephesians 4:11-13.

> *So Christ himself gave the apostle, the prophets, the evangelists, the pastors and teachers, to equip his people for works of service, so that the body of Christ may be built up until we all reach unity in the faith and in the knowledge of the Son of God and become mature, attaining to the whole measure of the fullness of Christ.*

Paul says that APEST is given primarily to equip the body of Christ to do works of service. Opening ourselves up to being equipped by the other giftings presents us with a unique opportunity to grow in our relationship with Christ. By leaving your Base ministry and entering a Phase of equipping, you will begin to enter into new dimensions of Christ's ministry. If you enter a Phase of evangelistic ministry, you will be entering into a part of Christ's ministry as an evangelist. You will experience his life and ministry in ways you have never experienced before.

APEST allows us to participate with Christ in ways that otherwise would be impossible. Without prophets, we would not know how to participate in the prophetic aspects of Christ's ministry. Without apostles, we would not know how to fully imitate the missional nature of Christ's life. Without teachers, we would not grow in our appreciation for the teachings of Jesus.

Each gifting gives us access to a measure of Christ that otherwise we would not have. We truly are the body of Christ, placed in relationship with one another to represent Christ to each other and to the world around us.

Ask the Lord to help you enter into a Phase of ministry that will help you experience and participate in that part of Christ's ministry.

// APEST and Collective Intelligence

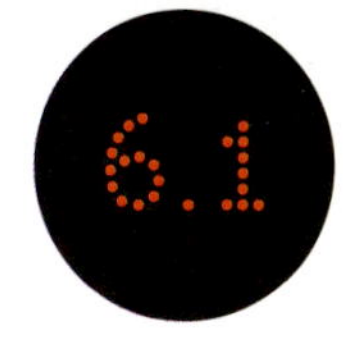

The great thing about broadening our vision toward a five-fold understanding of ministry is that we open ourselves up to a new way of seeing. Each APEST ministry has a unique perspective to contribute. They each bring a certain kind of intelligence, as it were, to the table. And this collective intelligence gives each group the adaptive resources it needs to effectively face its challenges.

The tricky part about opening the group to multiple perspectives is that things can get confusing and complicated. Awakening diversity in a group can also pose a challenge to the group's sense of unity. How do you awaken diversity in the group while still maintaining a healthy and productive sense of unity? We have found that groups can leverage diversity for positive outcomes by going through a process known as *fit, split, contend and transcend.** This process is designed to help groups develop creative solutions to challenging problems. Let's see what it looks like.

*Richard T. Pascale, *Managing on the Edge: How Successful Companies Use Conflict to Stay Ahead* (Simon and Schuster: New York, 1990).

Fit, split, contend, transcend

Fit

In order for this process to work, your group has to start from a place of unity. This means your group should have a sense of clarity about where they are going—vision—and why they are going there—values. These two things function like a center of gravity to keep the group together. Starting from a place of unity includes affirming a sense of mutual love for God, each other, the church community and your city. It's bonding time, so let lots of love flow as you begin this process.

COACHING MOMENT

Most people join a group after its vision and values have been determined. If this is the case with most of the people in your group, it would be wise to revisit your vision and values to make sure everyone is on the same page. However, if your current group has not determined its vision and values, or if there is significant confusion about what they are, then we strongly suggest you spend the proper amount of time working to shape those. If you awaken the diversity of perspectives in the group without first having unity about each other and your collective vision and values, you will likely get stuck somewhere between the next two phases, Split and Contend.

Split

Split refers to the practice of creating space in the group to entertain different perspectives. Because each APEST gifting reflects a different focus of Christ's ministry, each group contains the potential to approach various topics and tasks from multiple angles. Encouraging a diversity of expression opens the group to a wider perspective, limiting potential blind spots.

Contend

If *split* was about populating the canvas with the various APEST perspectives, the *contend* phase is about formulating a solution out of those perspectives. At this phase, everyone steps back into their individual roles in the group and begins the process of working toward a meaningful solution.

There is real tension at this phase. The different perspectives generated during *split* all represent a different facet of reality, and these different ways of seeing will generate tension and conflict. However, tension can be a good thing if it is managed well.

COACHING MOMENT

The Split Exercise allows you to tap into the variety of capacities already present within the group. It forces you to look at a problem from all angles, which allows for a more adaptive solution to emerge. In order for this to happen, the group has to give each other permission to disagree, debate and dialogue in order to reach creative solutions.

The mark of an effective group is not the absence of conflict, but rather their ability to work creatively through conflict in ways that honor and respect one another and God (see Ephesians 4:1-3).

Transcend

Through the guidance of a group leader, the group can begin to move toward a solution that takes into account the unity of the group (Fit), as well as the various facets of reality surrounding the challenge at hand (Split). The goal is not to opt for one APEST perspective above the others, but to incorporate each one into the decision-making process in ways that allow you to see both the forest (Fit) and the trees (Split).

Notes

Each phase of *fit, split, contend, and transcend* will resonate differently with each one of us. Affirming the unity of the group (Fit) will be an enjoyable event for some. Others will get excited about the opportunity to explore topics and tasks from multiple perspectives (Split). As strange as this may sound, some people will actually be energized by vibrant discussions and debates (Contend). Others will find great satisfaction by bringing closure and arriving at a plan to move forward (Transcend).

Which phase of this process sounds the most enjoyable to you?

Which phase do you think would be the least enjoyable? Explain.

Why do you think going through a process like this would be beneficial for your group?

MEDITATION // APEST and Collective Intelligence

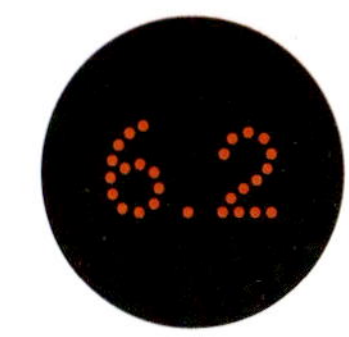

At times, wrestling through different perspectives can make you feel like you are being stretched to your limits. While your group should not live in this kind of tension, periodically visiting these places of tension can prove to be a fertile experience. In Ephesians 4:25-32, Paul provides some great principles about how we should navigate this tension to ensure it is channeled toward a healthy and productive experience. Read this passage slowly and carefully.

> *Therefore each of you must put off falsehood and speak truthfully to your neighbor, for we are all members of one body. "In your anger do not sin": Do not let the sun go down while you are still angry, and do not give the devil a foothold. Anyone who has been stealing must steal no longer, but must work, doing something useful with their own hands, that they may have something to share with those in need. Do not let any unwholesome talk come out of your mouths, but only what is helpful for building others up according to their needs, that it may benefit those who listen. And do not grieve the Holy Spirit of God, with whom you were sealed for the day of redemption. Get rid of all bitterness, rage and anger, brawling and slander, along with every form of malice. Be kind and compassionate to one another, forgiving each other, just as in Christ God forgave you.*

In this passage, Paul gives us great guidance on how to navigate the tensions that can emerge during the phases of *split* and *contend*. The following pages explain this further.

Passage 4:25

Topic: Lying

Task: Speak truth to one another, be open and honest about your perspectives

Phase(s) of the Process This Applies to:
Split and contend

Passage 4:26a

Topic: Anger

Task: Express yourself, but do not sin against group members

Phase(s) of the Process This Applies to:
Contend

Passage 4:26b

Topic: Anger

Task: Do not hold grudges against group members

Phase(s) of the Process This Applies to:
Contend

Passage 4:27

Topic: Spiritual Warfare

Task: Do not give the Devil an opportunity to influence you or the group by mismanaging your anger

Phase(s) of the Process This Applies to:
Contend

Passage 4:29

Topic: Talk

Task: Look for ways to build up people in the group, not tear them down

Phase(s) of the Process This Applies to:
Split and contend

Passage 4:30-32

Topic: Forgiveness

Task: Forgive people in your group when they offend you

Phase(s) of the Process This Applies to:
Split and contend

The challenges most groups face center on living in the tension between unity and diversity. *Fit, split, contend, and transcend* provides a way to navigate those tensions. But in order for that process to be productive, it has to be guided by the principles in Ephesians 4:25-32. Since most of the tension in a group surfaces during *split* and *contend*, the following questions will help focus your attention around the topics and tasks revealed in this passage of Scripture.

Notes

O LORD, who shall sojourn in your tent? Who shall dwell on your holy hill? He who walks blamelessly and does what is right and speaks truth in his heart; who does not slander with his tongue and does no evil to his neighbor, nor takes up a reproach against his friend. **(Psalm 15:1–3 ESV)**

The word translated *lie* in Ephesians 4:25 is the Greek word *pseudo*, which can also mean to give a false impression. This word shows us that lying might mean being inauthentic instead of true to who we are. Other times lying happens when it just seems easier to pretend like we agree with something in order to avoid conflict in the group.

Listen to the reason Paul gives for why we should not give false impressions to one another: We are members of one another. In other words, we are on the same team!

Do you tend to share your thoughts and feelings with your group, or do you tend to keep them to yourself?

Why?

Each one of us brings a different perspective into the group. Creating space where we can share this kind of diversity requires each person in the group to practice the art of listening to one another.

On a scale of 1 to 10, how are you when it comes to listening to the perspectives of other people in your group?

Do Not Listen — Attentive Listener

1 2 3 4 5 6 7 8 9 10

The *split* and *contend* phases are designed to give each team member a safe place to express their disagreements with one another and to voice their alternative perspectives. When this happens, we can sometimes be offended by what our group members say or even how they say it. According to Paul, suppressing our anger and holding grudges gives room for the devil to operate.

When you are offended, do you tend to hold a grudge or seek to resolve it as soon as possible? Why?

One of the ways a group can lose its sense of unity is through sarcasm. Too much fun at the expense of others will erode trust and respect between people. Paul says that we should be looking for opportunities to build one another up so we can be channels of grace to one another.

Where would you place yourself on this continuum?

Are you overly sarcastic, overly serious or somewhere in between? Where you are being sensitive to the needs of those around you?

There is one whose rash words are like sword thrusts, but the tongue of the wise brings healing. **(Proverbs 12:18 ESV)**

Overly Sarcastic   Sensitive   Overly Serious

1 2 3 4 5 6 7 8 9 10

Working toward being a better group starts with working toward being a better *member* of the group.

If you could pick one task from the table above (pg. 132-133), which do you feel is most relevant to your growth as a group member?

Write it down and ask the Father to help you change your way of thinking, being and doing in this area.

Mark Conner, a friend of mine (Alan) and a leader of Citylife church in Melbourne, Australia, is deeply committed to building his leaders into a team that appreciates and values each person's differences and unique perspectives. Here is one of the team exercises he uses to illustrate the importance of diversity:

Mark places an object (say, a statue) in the middle of a round table and asks people to share what they see. He notes that three things happen. First, everyone sees the object differently. Second, no one sees it accurately because each one sees it from where he or she sits. And finally, the only way everyone can see it accurately is when each person listens to everyone else's perspective. This exercise shows that without multiple perspectives we cannot develop an accurate view of the challenges and opportunities in front of us. This is true in every area of life and ministry—problem-solving, decision-making, vision creation, and strategic planning.

The *fit, split, contend, and transcend* process is designed to engage your group in disciplines that foster growth and maturity. For example, a group may have developed a great *fit*, but may not know how to *contend* with one another in healthy, productive ways. Depending on the makeup of your group, conflict may cause some to get overly defensive or even shut down and withdraw from participating in group discussions. Others may become overly aggressive, resorting to personal attacks or name calling. These are all signs that a group is ripe for learning how to speak the truth in love.

Working through this exercise of *fit, split, contend, and transcend* will not only highlight your strengths as a group, it will also force your weaknesses out into the open. But remember, healthy groups emerge out of the process of wrestling with the tension that comes from embracing both unity and diversity. Your own growth and maturity as a group member will be linked directly to your willingness to open yourself to each phase of this process. The same is true for the group as a whole. The following questions will help you think about where you as a group member are in relation to each phase of this process.

Therefore confess your sins to each other and pray for each other so that you may be healed. The prayer of a righteous person is powerful and effective. **(James 5:16)**

Notes

Fit

Vision: As a group member, how clear are you about where the group is trying to go?

Mark a place on the continuum that best describes illustrates your level of clarity.

In the Dark. . . . . .Fuzzy. . . . . Crystal Clear

Write down the revelation and make it plain on tablets so that a herald may run with it. **(Habakkuk 2:2b)**

Values: As a group member, how clear are you about why the group wants to go there?

Mark a place on the continuum that best illustrates your level of clarity.

In the Dark. . . . . .Fuzzy. . . . . Crystal Clear

I appeal to you, brothers and sisters, in the name of our Lord Jesus Christ, that all of you agree with one another in what you say and that there be no divisions among you, but that you be perfectly united in mind and thought. **(1 Corinthians 1:10)**

Write out what you currently understand your group's vision and values to be. If you're not sure, just guess based on your experience in the group. You will be asked to share this on Synergy Day.

Split

Some people prefer to reach solutions quickly with minimal effort, dialogue or disagreement. Listening to various group members explain their perspectives takes time. It requires a lot of listening and presses the boundaries of our imagination.

Know this, my beloved brothers: let every person be quick to hear, slow to speak, slow to anger; for the anger of man does not produce the righteousness of God. **(James 1:19–20 ESV)**

When it comes to listening, which one of these phrases best describes the way you listen to other people? Explain your answer.

I'm sorry—did you say something?

Why are we still talking about this?

Would you let me finish?!

Yes, that's exactly what I am saying!

Does anyone else have something to say?

The one who has knowledge uses words with restraint, and whoever has understanding is even-tempered. **(Proverbs 17:27)**

Contend

The *contend* phase is difficult for most people because it forces people to work through conflict.

*Which word best describes your approach to dealing with conflict?**

Avoiding: You neglect your own concerns and the concerns of others

Accommodating: You neglect your own concerns to satisfy the concerns of others

Competing: You prioritize your own concerns above the concerns of others

Compromising: You look for a solution that partially satisfies your own concerns as well as the concerns of group members

Collaborating: You work toward a solution that takes into account the concerns of all, yet prioritizes the vision and values of the team.

Never be wise in your own sight. Repay no one evil for evil, but give thought to do what is honorable in the sight of all. If possible, so far as it depends on you, live peaceably with all.
(Romans 12:16b-18 ESV)

*These categories are taken from the insightful work of Kenneth W. Thomas and Ralph H. Kilmann in the Thomas-Kilmann Conflict Mode Instrument (CPP, Inc.: 2002).

May the God who gives endurance and encouragement give you the same attitude of mind toward each other that Christ Jesus had, so that with one mind and one voice you may glorify the God and Father of our Lord Jesus Christ. **(Romans 15:5-6)**

Transcend
Transcending is what happens when you are able to pass through each phase of the process and arrive at a solution that takes into account both the forest and the trees.

What has been your experience with groups you have been a part of in the past? How often have they been able to arrive at solutions that transcend the common mistakes of missing the forest for the trees or the trees for the forest?

Explain.

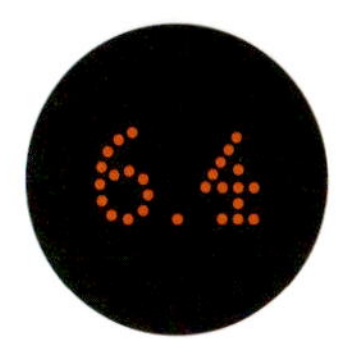

Your success as an individual is not tied up in your ability to avoid conflict. If anything, conflict will be the place we learn our most valuable lessons. The thing that will determine the long-term health of your group will be its willingness to submit to the teachings of Scripture on how to handle conflict.

Today is going to be a tough action step. More than likely, if you have been in a group for any significant amount of time, you have been offended by someone in that group. If you have not been offended, then you have likely (intentionally or unintentionally) been the offender. Regardless of which scenario applies, Scripture is clear as to how we are to respond in each situation.

If you have been offended, then you need to start working through the implications of Matthew 18:15-20 with the person who has offended you.

If you have been the one who has offended someone else (whether intentionally or unintentionally) then you need to work through the implications of Matthew 5:23-24 with the person you have offended.

While working through the implications of these passages may take some time, we want to challenge you to begin the process today by owning up to the reality of the situation and committing to talk with the person you offended or who offended you as soon as possible. Learning how to work through conflict is both critical to the health of the body and to your own health as a disciple of Jesus Christ. Email, call or text someone today to set up a time to resolve the conflict.

Offend(ed)

If your brother sins against you, go and show him his fault, just between the two of you. If he listens to you, you have won your brother over. But if he will not listen, take one or two others along, so that "every matter may be established by the testimony of two or three witnesses." If he refuses to listen to them, tell it to the church; and if he refuses to listen even to the church, treat him as you would a pagan or a tax collector. I tell you the truth, whatever you bind on earth will be bound in heaven, and whatever you loose on earth will be loosed in heaven. Again, I tell you that if two of you on earth agree about anything you ask for, it will be done for you by my Father in heaven. For where two or three come together in my name, there am I with them. (Matthew 18:15-20 ESV)

Offend(er)

Therefore, if you are offering your gift at the altar and there remember that your brother or sister has something against you, leave your gift there in front of the altar. First go and be reconciled to them; then come and offer your gift. (Matthew 5:23-24)

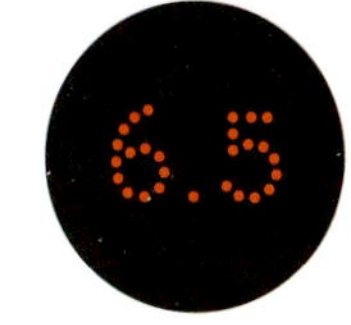

This week, we have focused on how to engage the diversity of perspectives within APEST. One way to draw these different perspectives into the open is to use a problem-solving tool developed by Edward de Bono called Thinking Hats.* A "hat" represents a certain mode of thinking. The approach requires everyone to change perspectives and focus their conversation in accordance with the hat being worn at the moment. Everyone can contribute to the conversation based on the kind of thinking called for by the particular hat.

Thinking Hat Colors
Blue: visionary
White: facts
Green: creative
Red: caution
Black: critical
Yellow: feelings

*E. de Bono, *Serious Creativity: Using the Power of Lateral Thinking to Create New Ideas* (New York: Harper Business, 1993).

APEST "Thinking Hats"

Applying this to Ephesians 4, each category of APEST could represent a particular hat that focuses the group's thinking and conversation. The group selects a particular challenge and considers it together using each APEST hat. When putting a hat on, the team is only allowed to process and discuss the challenge at hand through that hat. So if you're wearing the apostolic hat, you should respond from an apostolic perspective—for example, interests related to missional extension, organizational integrity and design, and guarding the overarching sustainability of the venture. Next, you might put the prophet hat on and focus the group's attention around prophetic concerns and sensibilities, and so on. Wrestling through opposing viewpoints forces the team to think outside the box and approach topics from new angles, allowing the group to see their challenges from multiple angles. This exercise sets in motion certain aspects of Base and Phase that force people to stretch their imaginations.

Group Exercise: APEST Thinking Hats

To make this exercise easier and less threatening, we have provided an imaginary scenario. Have someone in the group read this scenario out loud. Then, using the APEST Thinking Hats exercise outlined above, explore this scenario from all five APEST perspectives. Note particular concerns and opportunities related to each perspective.

***Scenario:* STEPHANIE**

Stephanie walks into the group meeting and says she has something to tell the group about Caroline. Stephanie met Caroline about 2½ months ago in line at the grocery store. After some small talk, they ended up sharing some of their stories with one another in the parking lot. Caroline told Stephanie that she was abandoned by her family at an early age. While in foster care, Caroline eventually got involved in a gang and ended up getting arrested for car theft. She spent the next three years in a local juvenile detention center. At age 18, Caroline was released from detention and has been struggling ever since. Caroline is now 22 years old and looking for a job. Stephanie invited her to come to your weekly group meeting, and to her surprise, Caroline showed up the next week and started coming on a weekly basis.

After a month of being in the group, Caroline approached the group about a financial need for transportation. She had a job offer on the other side of town but needed a car to make it to and from work. The group responded by collecting enough money to help Caroline purchase a used car and paid for the first six months of insurance. Caroline was really grateful.

It has now been three months since Caroline has been hanging out with the group on a weekly basis. Recently, Caroline made it known to Stephanie that she is in need of some more money. This time, she needs help with paying her rent. She is three months behind and they are threatening to evict her. Stephanie tells the group about Caroline's need and is convinced the group should help her again. Stephanie does, however, let the group know that Caroline has a boyfriend living in her apartment at the moment, something Caroline has never mentioned.

Stephanie has met with Caroline twice in the past two months to pray and study the Bible. When the group asked Stephanie if Caroline had found a job she told them that Caroline found one, but was recently fired because she called in sick one day. Stephanie says Caroline has not been looking for a job because she has no way of getting around.

Additional Facts:
Caroline has not shown up to the group meeting for the past two weeks.

Caroline's boyfriend is unemployed.

Caroline has a daughter that she did not tell the group about—but Stephanie knows about it.

Everyone in the group is a Christian, but Caroline is not.

Should the group help Caroline with her rent?

If yes, why and how?

If no, why not and how?

The goal of this exercise is to learn how to draw out and listen to the different APEST perspectives within your group so you can approach challenges from a more well-rounded, less biased perspective. After you explore this scenario using the APEST Thinking Hats exercise, answer the following questions.

Notes

What are some areas the group did well in as they explored the different APEST perspectives regarding the challenge?

What were some of the challenges the group faced while discussing this scenario from the different APEST perspectives?

Most likely, someone said something in the discussion that made you see things a little differently. Go around the group and have each person mention who enhanced his or her perspective, and how. What was that person's primary APEST ministry? How do you think this shaped their perspective?

If you had to do this exercise again, what would you do differently?

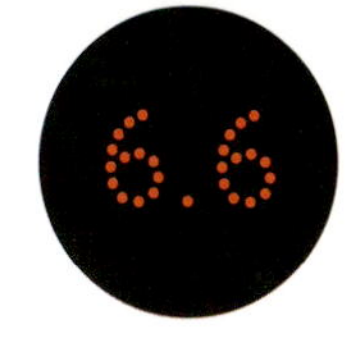

The process of *fit, split, contend, and transcend* helps you engage the diversity of APEST within the group while at the same time working toward a practical place of unity. It's not always easy to go through this process, but it allows us the opportunity to engage in certain aspects of Base and Phase ministry. It causes us to hold the tension between unity and diversity that helps us move toward growth and maturity.

Yet we have to emphasize this critical truth: Regardless of how well APEST is represented in the group, the energy for a permanent revolution will remain dormant if the group does not learn how to embrace the unique perspectives of each group member. Unity in diversity starts with each person being open to the other person's perspective. This kind of openness is only sustainable if we are willing to speak the truth in love. Love is what ultimately holds the group together and allows it to work through a process like *fit, split, contend, and transcend.* If love is present, the group can come out on the other side of the process more fully equipped to represent the ministry of Christ.

In order to make this practical, let's look at what Paul says about love in I Corinthians 13:4-8.

> *Love is patient, love is kind. It does not envy, it does not boast, it is not proud. It does not dishonor others, it is not self-seeking, it is not easily angered, it keeps no record of wrongs. Love does not delight in evil but rejoices with the truth. It always protects, always trusts, always hopes, always perseveres. Love never fails...*

The goal of this command is love, which comes from a pure heart and a good conscience and a sincere faith. **(1 Timothy 1:5)**

Can you imagine what your group would be like if this kind of love were present between group members? Unity in diversity can exist if we are willing to bear with one another in love.

Notes

But the Lord is faithful, and he will strengthen you and protect you from the evil one. We have confidence in the Lord that you are doing and will continue to do the things we command. May the Lord direct your hearts into God's love and Christ's perseverance. **(2 Thessalonians 3:3–5)**

Ephesians 4:7-16 is primarily about growing in our competencies for ministry. But growing in the competencies of Christ (ministry skills) without growing in the character of Christ (attitude and motivations) is not real growth and maturity. It is our love for one another that allows us to go through a process where we can develop both our character and competency for representing the fullness of Christ.

End your time today praying that the Father would increase your love for the people in your group.

As we end this learning experience, we want to revisit the promise of Ephesians 3:20-21:

> *Now to him who is able to do immeasurably more than all we ask or imagine, according to his power that is at work within us, to him be glory in the church and in Christ Jesus throughout all generations, for ever and ever! Amen.*

We are destined to be a permanent revolution, a transformative force that works its way through every sphere of society and culture, exposing God's glory from generation to generation. God really can do more than we ask or imagine. His design is to unleash this transformative power in and through us, the church, the body of Christ. Through the strengthening of his Spirit in our inner being, through the unity we have in Christ and the diversity of ministries through APEST, the body of Christ grows and matures into the fullness of Christ in the world. We have been given to each other as gifts to represent the revolutionary ministry of Christ. And as with all of God's gifts, we are invited to respond.

Will you receive yourself as a gift? Will you receive your group members as a gift? Will you open yourself up to the diversity within APEST so you can be equipped to represent the full spectrum of Christ's ministry? If so, let the permanent revolution begin...

> *I pray that out of his glorious riches he may strengthen you with power through his Spirit in your inner being.* (Ephesians 3:16)

The Permanent Revolution: Apostolic Imagination and Practice for the 21st Century Church

by Alan Hirsch & Tim Catchim

Available on amazon.com

The *Permanent Revolution* is an original work of theological reimagination and reconstruction that draws from biblical studies, theology, organizational theory, leadership studies and key social sciences. The book elaborates on the apostolic role rooted in the five-fold ministry from Ephesians 4 (apostles, prophets, evangelists, shepherds and teachers), and its significance for the missional movement.

Throughout the book, the authors propose a revolutionary missional ecclesiology that is shaped by the New Testament account of apostolic imagination, ministry and strategy. The aim is to reclaim the ministry by which the church is to remain centered on its calling to be the instrument of God's mission, and that everything it is and does ought to relate to and demonstrate that calling. To (re)capture the practice of apostolicity, the authors explore how the apostolic ministry facilitates ongoing renewal in the life of the church and focus on leadership in relation to missional innovation and entrepreneurship. They examine the nature of organization as reframed through the lens of apostolic ministry and explore how apostolic leadership provides new and missionally creative ways forward.

The *Permanent Revolution* is filled with challenging concepts and is replete with innovative ideas. Rather than providing a prescriptive model for leadership, it offers spiritual prods and suggestive thought experiments that are designed to stimulate imagination as well as action. If faithful leaders are to take up the work of ministry as laid out in the New Testament, this book offers a significant pathway to help equip them to better fulfill their mission.

APEST MINISTRY PROFILE TEST

		Often	Sometimes	Rarely
1	I am good at listening and taking in what people say.			
2	People say I am good at presenting information and ideas.			
3	When I'm excited about something, I get others interested in it too.			
4	I can accurately assess a person based on first impressions and know instinctively if they are being real with me.			
5	I can be counted on to contribute original ideas.			
6	I see more value in building up something meaningful and useful than always striking out into new initiatives.			
7	I try explaining things in different ways if people are finding a concept difficult to grasp or understand.			
8	People with different value systems have said that they feel comfortable when they are around me, and that I have a positive effect on them being open to new ideas.			
9	People describe me as entrepreneurial.			
10	When I communicate truth (even hard truth) to others I see resulting changes in their knowledge, attitudes, values or conduct.			
11	I like to tell stories, especially my own.			
12	I like to create safe places for people to flourish and grow.			
13	I like to share what I believe.			
14	Sometimes I just intuitively know things that others seem to miss.			
15	I can clarify goals, develop strategies and cast a vision to accomplish tasks.			
16	I remember names or at least where I first met someone.			
17	I generally appreciate hard facts more than theories.			
18	I have enjoyed relating to a certain group of people over a period of time, sharing personally in their successes and their failures.			
19	I sometimes get frustrated and even depressed at the lack of faith or understanding of others around me.			
20	I like change even when it makes others uncomfortable.			
21	I am able to discern the real meaning behind things.			

		Often	Sometimes	Rarely
22	I love to show people how to do things that I do well.			
23	I sometimes feel compelled to speak the truth, even if it makes others feel uncomfortable.			
24	I enjoy coming up with new and original ideas, dreaming big and thinking about visions for the future.			
25	I like to provide a safe and comfortable environment where people feel they are welcome, that they belong, are listened to and cared for.			
26	I enjoy meditation and thinking deeply about spiritual things.			
27	I've always wanted to build a business/organization from the ground up so I can give my specific vision to it.			
28	I am faithful in providing support, care and nurture for others over long periods of time, even when others have stopped.			
29	I have expressed my spiritual feelings as pictures or analogies.			
30	I enjoy taking notes when someone is speaking and pay close attention to the details of what they are saying.			
31	I like to help organizations, groups and leaders become more efficient and often find myself thinking about how things function.			
32	When I like a movie or a restaurant, everyone will hear about it.			
33	People tell me that the things I say often help them to try new things.			
34	I enjoy coming up with the best, most efficient way to do a task right.			
35	Social justice for the poor and marginalized means a great deal to me.			
36	I don't shy away from controversial subjects if they are important to me.			
37	I enjoy digging out information, ideas and metaphors to explain a concept.			
38	Sometimes, in my enthusiasm, I push my views too far with people.			
39	I have a clear vision, and others have said that they feel confident to go along with me.			
40	I try to think of different ways of expressing the truth.			
41	I regularly like to be alone for long periods of time to reflect and think.			
42	I empathize with those who are hurting or broken and can support them through their pain to wholeness.			
43	When reading, it is easier for me to grasp the wider picture or message than the specific details.			

APEST MINISTRY PROFILE TEST - Score Sheet

#	Often	Sometimes	Rarely
1			
6			
8			
10			
12			
16			
18			
25			
28			
42			
Total marked "Often":		x 2 =	
Total marked "Sometimes":			
SHEPHERD Total:			

#	Often	Sometimes	Rarely
2			
6			
7			
10			
17			
22			
30			
34			
37			
40			
Total marked "Often":		x 2 =	
Total marked "Sometimes":			
TEACHER Total:			

#	Often	Sometimes	Rarely
3			
8			
11			
13			
16			
18			
32			
36			
38			
40			
Total marked "Often":		x 2 =	
Total marked "Sometimes":			
EVANGELIST Total:			

#	Often	Sometimes	Rarely
4			
14			
19			
21			
23			
26			
29			
35			
36			
41			
Total marked "Often":		x 2 =	
Total marked "Sometimes":			
PROPHET Total:			

#	Often	Sometimes	Rarely
5			
9			
15			
20			
24			
27			
31			
33			
39			
43			
Total marked "Often":		x 2 =	
Total marked "Sometimes":			
APOSTLE Total:			

This APEST Ministry Profile Test is adapted from the 5 Fold Ministry Survey which is © 3DM and Mike Breen. To access the full version please visit weare3dm.com/store.

If you're looking for a more in-depth comprehensive test for personal and group APEST Ministry profiles, you can find an online APEST Assessment at www.apest.org.

Resources by Missio and Missio Publishing

The story of Missio is described in detail in *The Tangible Kingdom: Creating Incarnational Community* by Hugh Halter and Matt Smay. The book has a companion guide called the *Tangible Kingdom Primer* which is designed to help Christians, churches, and small groups get on the pathway of spiritual formation and missional engagement. The primer creates opportunities to experience authentic missional community. It leads participants on a challenging eight week journey toward an incarnational lifestyle and moves far beyond the typical small group experience.

Brandon Hatmaker's book *Barefoot Church* and the corresponding resource the *Barefoot Church Primer* tell the next chapter in the Missio story. The *Barefoot Church Primer* provides practical steps toward living out the good news of Jesus in a world full of need. The primer creates a unique opportunity to invite Christians from all backgrounds as well as non-Christian friends to join you in serving the least. The eight week study works to naturally create a wealth of missional ministry openings as an outcome of learning to serve the least together.

The Gospel Primer by Caesar Kalinowski will help you creatively answer the question: what is the Gospel? The primer examines the Story of God as found in scripture and teaches the reader to form a personal Gospel Story in a natural, yet powerful way. *The Gospel Primer* is designed to help any group of people cultivate a practical understanding of the gospel and grow in gospel fluency—the ability to proclaim and demonstrate the gospel in every area of life. This unique resource will help you gain a deep understanding and practice of the Gospel.

Missio Publishing is committed to resourcing the church with practical tools to help it engage more effectively in missional and incarnational ministry.

To purchase the primers and other resources, along with bulk discounts for churches, visit **www.missiopublishing.com**.

APEST
Ministry
Profile Test